From Arthur's Seat

Editor in Chief	Magali Román
Executive Editor	Merel de Beer
Art Director	Elspeth Reilly
Editorial Board (prose)	Amanda-Marie Kale
	Natasha Grodzinski
	Milagros Lasarte
	John Reid
	Elena Sims
	Wester Wagenaar
Editorial Board (poetry)	Dexter Yim
	Ellie Jackson
	Elspeth Reilly
	Stefano Paparo
Copy Editor	Nicole Christine Caratas
Proofreaders	C. Maris Bounds
	Nicole Hooper Campos
	Stefano Paparo
Web Manager	Natasha Grodzinski
Social Media Manager	Sophie Lay
Podcast Producer	Wester Wagenaar
Podcast Narrator	John Reid
Event Planners	Alyssa Osiecki
	Julie Galante
Special Thanks	Jane McKie
	Claire Askew
	Katie Craig
	Jane Alexander
	Robert Alan Jamieson
	Alan Gillis
	Allyson Stack

Table of Contents

How To Read This Book *Magali Román*	8
Foreword *Dr Claire Askew*	10

Prose

Athenaeum *Magali Román*	14
He Was Always Hers *C. Maris Bounds*	17
Neighbourly Compassion *Sophie Lay*	24
Fear of Missing Out *Natasha Grodzinski*	31
Will of the Wisp *Issa Dioume*	40
From the Ceiling *M.E. Gerretsen*	50
Of Relative Colours *Angelo Castiglioni*	57
The Club *Julie Galante*	64
Sparks *Alyssa Osiecki*	68
In the Attic *Elena Sims*	75

Cracks
Wester Wagenaar 83

The (Beep)
Milagros Lasarte 90

Diggin
Iona Zawinski 98

Alveolus
Josh Wagner 105

Vex Hex
Ning Cai 113

The Fox is in the Wing of Sector Y
Ning Cai 119

To the Moon
Nicole Christine Caratas 121

Atqasuk
Marc Berry 129

Chinatown
TingYu Li 135

The Immortal Science
James Alex 143

How it Ends
Nicole Hooper Campos 148

Plan for the You To-Do Tomorrow
Amanda-Marie Kale 156

I Don't Think I Can Be Your Writer Anymore
Amanda-Marie Kale 162

Excerpts

Mint Castle
John Reid — 169

A Dance With the Devil
Kirsty Souter — 175

Poetry

To Edinburgh with Love
Ning Cai — 186

Secret Base
Dexter Yim — 188

Kintsugi
Dexter Yim — 189

Murphy's Law
Dexter Yim — 190

The Museum of Childhood
Ellie Jackson — 192

speckled brains
Ellie Jackson — 194

sunday afternoon
Ellie Jackson — 195

against the bank, asleep
Stefano Paparo — 196

asteroid
Stefano Paparo — 197

what got me
Stefano Paparo — 198

Fledgling *Elspeth Reilly*	200
Soap Lady *Elspeth Reilly*	202
The Usual *Elspeth Reilly*	204
Our Garden of Love *Ali Musa Ame*	206
Unyago Song *Ali Musa Ame*	207
The Lion in the Royal Emblem *Ali Musa Ame*	208

Prizewinners

SLOAN PRIZE Clairvoyant *Charles Lang*	212
GRIERSON VERSE PRIZE Tritina for my India *Alycia Pirmohamed*	213
LEWIS EDWARDS MEMORIAL PRIZE Sunday Breakfast *Snigdha Koirala*	214

Biographies

Team and Writers	220
A Note On The Design	228

How to Read this Book

From Arthur's Seat is an anthology of short prose and poetry from twenty-nine emerging writers and poets, consisting of twenty-three short stories, sixteen poems, and two excerpts from longer works. As such, this book contains a wide variety of stories, and it has been structured to be read in two different ways.

The first is the traditional cover-to-cover order; with three sections containing short prose, excerpts, and poetry. The reader may choose to read the entire volume in order, according to their own wishes.

The second method involves following an unusual set of instructions. You may notice that the final page of each story and poem is marked by a coordinate. These coordinates chart separate "paths" that link together three to five stories and poems, to reveal secret overarching narratives hidden inside this anthology. There are ten paths in total, and ten stories to discover. The reader may find, as they follow each path, that many of these seemingly disparate tales transform into unconventional companion pieces.

The reader may follow a path by tracing the coordinates (X, Y) stamped at the bottom center of the final page of each story or poem, with X representing the path number it belongs to and Y representing the page number on which the succeeding story can be found. To follow path X simply flip to the page number outlined in Y.

(X, Y) = (path number, page number)

In creating these alternative paths, this volume of From Arthur's Seat puts choice in the hands of you, the reader. Its purpose is not to create a gimmick, but rather to suggest new ways of reading the multilayered stories in this anthology. No matter which path you choose, we hope you enjoy your adventure.

Magali Román, Editor in Chief

Table of Instructions

To start, pick a path from the ten options below. Begin at the page number specified by the first coordinate and follow the sets of coordinates until you reach the end of each path.

Path I: A Word from Your Author A narrator looks for a story
(1, 14), (1, 169), (1, 105), (1, 202), (1, 162).

Path II: Mystery of Love Stories of love and loss
(2, 186), (2,17), (2, 206), (2, 83), (2, 64), (2, 195).

Path III: Going Slightly Mad A woman loses control
(3, 156), (3, 31), (3, 90), (3, 196).

Path IV: Breaking the Surface An eerie crime comes to light
(4, 198), (4, 40), (4, 194), (4, 98).

Path V: Lunar Phases Stories of power and celestial bodies
(5, 68), (5, 121), (5, 197).

Path VI: Museum of Childhood Stories of childhood, both conventional and not.
(6, 192), (6, 50), (6, 188), (6, 135), (6, 207).

Path VII: A Legacy A speaker tries to preserve the image of a loved one
(7, 57), (7, 189), (7, 143), (7, 200).

Path VIII: Pandemonium Moments of absurd chaos, both in the world and in the mind
(8, 113), (8, 148), (8, 119).

Path IX: Neighbourhood Watch A community comes under surveillance
 (9, 175), (9, 204), (9, 24).

Path X: Ties That Bind War sinks its teeth in
(10, 75), (10, 190), (10, 129), (10, 208).

Foreword

Not everyone is a fan of creative writing Masters degrees. Creative writing can't be taught, say the critics. Masters degrees in creative writing result in generic fiction, generic poems, work written to a formula. Students of creative writing have chosen an easy qualification over the hard slog of gathering life experience. I once met an older male writer who looked me up and down and declared that my creative writing Masters – and by extension, my work – was "not worth the paper it was printed on."

I'd like to present this anthology, somewhat gleefully, as evidence to the contrary. The 2019 MSc Creative Writing cohort can – collectively, and as individuals – refute every one of those criticisms, and in this collection of work, it shows. This book features work by writers from all over the world, who bring huge variety to the page: the anthology showcases a wide range of ideas, experiences, genres, and styles. Many of the pieces speak to the anxiety and precarity of these times: Natasha Grodzinski's 'Fear of Missing Out,' and Nicole Hooper Campos's 'How It Ends' both provide their own take on the paranoia of living in a world where 24-hour news and social media disrupt the peace and grounding we might find in a more private sense of self. A still more malevolent surveillance appears in Sophie Lay's 'Neighbourly Compassion,' wherein a small community is made suddenly aware of a watchful presence in their midst. And many of us, whether writers or not, will recognise the quintessentially 21st century anxiety depicted by Amanda-Marie Kale's 'Plan for the You To-Do Tomorrow,' wherein the best intentions disintegrate into despair with more than a little help from Netflix, 'emails and social media and Facebook.'

Elsewhere, the book offers narratives that are timeless: for example, in 'Chinatown,' TingYu Li tells one family's story of sudden emigration that will chime with anyone who's ever had to uproot themselves and move far from home. In 'The Club,' Julie Galante writes sparely and with humour about the experience of losing a loved one to illness, finding a new twist on "death sucks" by looking through the lens of grief's massive, accompanying bureaucracy: 'there will be so much paperwork. And some grief, too. But mostly paperwork.' In the poetry section of the book, Elspeth Reilly's 'Fledgling' fizzes with so much empathy for strangers, the small details of their lives, that it almost hurts: 'everyone / could be my grandparents: / shaky hands, / finicky orders, / and winter coats still on.' Alyssa Osiecki deals with empathy, too, and the limits of it: in 'Sparks', a little girl suddenly discovers her own marvellous and dangerous power.

It has been a true privilege to work with this diverse and talented cohort of writers across their year of study. I have watched these students develop their ideas, hone their craft and commit over and over to becoming better, stronger writers. They truly dispel the myth that good writing is some sort of mystical superpower gifted to only a precious few. Good writing can be taught, can be learned, and the best students of writing craft know that the learning is never finished. This brilliant and multi-faceted anthology is only the first step for this cohort as they set out on a writing journey that I hope will be long, dedicated and fruitful.

I rest my case.

Dr Claire Askew
Writer in Residence
The University of Edinburgh

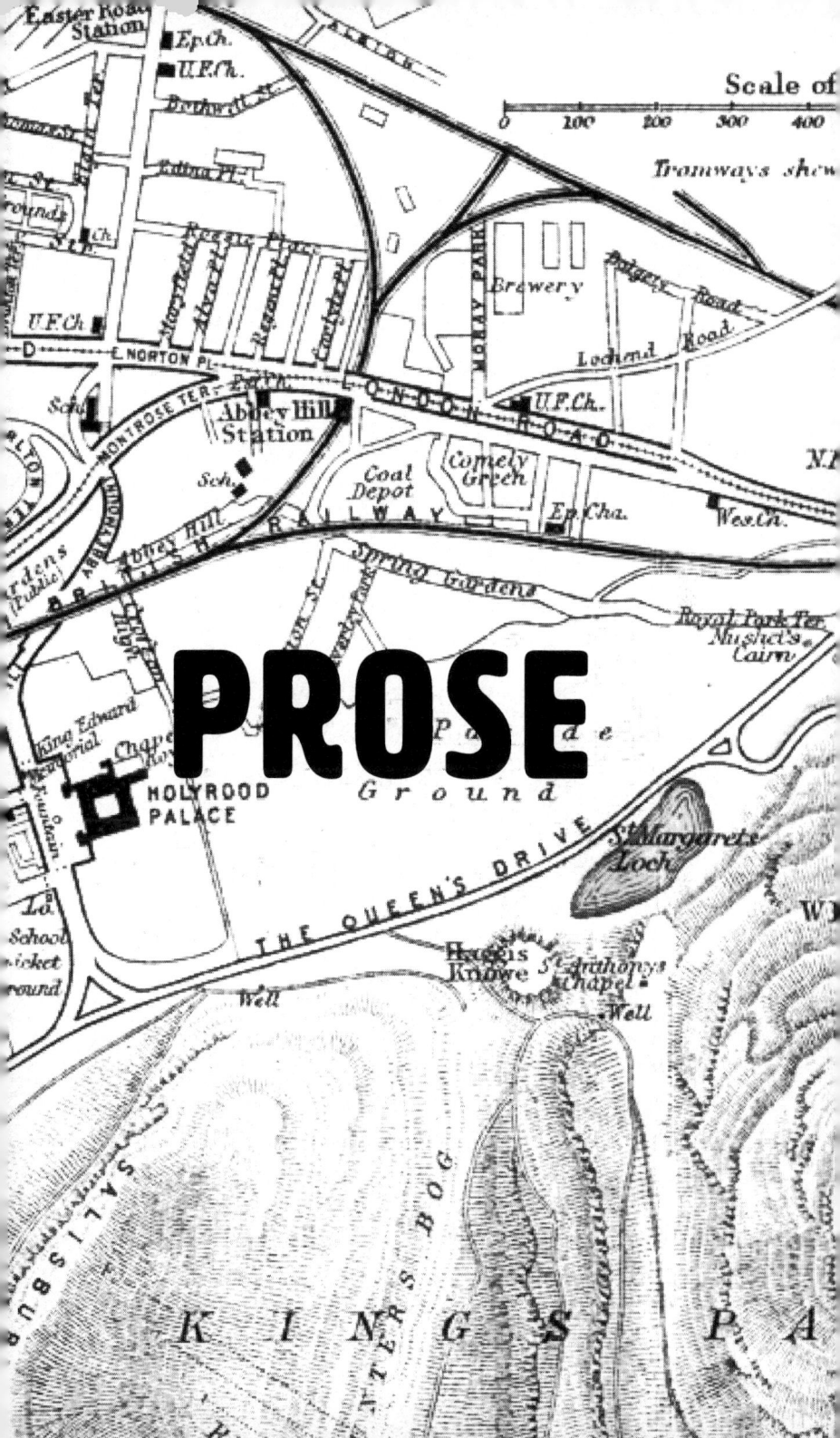

Athenaeum
Magali Román

There is a room where a man sits enclosed in darkness. The room is windowless and stale, closed off from the world with a door that can only be opened by a Visitor. The door is labeled with two names, neither of which are his. In truth, the man has no name. He only has a story.

Occasionally a Visitor will open the door and when this happens the man begins to speak. He delivers his testimony in layers: speaking first of a city, then a neighbourhood, then a family, and finally, a man. His tale spans a hundred years, yet it is told in just a few hours. It is important to divide the story into chapters, because you never know when a Visitor might grow tired and decide to close the door. The man speaks because he knows that speaking will keep the door open, and the longer the door stays open the stronger he becomes.

The man cannot see outside the room, but he can look upon the faces of his Visitors. He collects their eyes. They change all the time – sometimes they are young, sometimes they are old, and sometimes he catches only a glimpse before the Visitor slams the door shut and plunges him back into darkness. He thinks about these eyes in the dark. He holds onto their memory on the days when visits are scarce and the door opens so rarely that he grows weak and hungry. If nobody opened the door the man would not die, but he would become weak and unable to speak and for him that is worse than dying.

It is hard to guess how long a Visitor will stay. They are unpredictable creatures. Some of them cheer, chuckle, or gasp at crucial moments in the tale. Some Visitors even linger in the doorway, sighing in content bliss for hours on end, wasting away while the man, in turn, grows stronger. These are the best times. There are times when the door stays open for years and Visitors overcrowd the doorway, elbowing each other to listen in. Other times they shout, jeer, or slam the door in anger. On some occasions a Visitor listens, only to lock the door shut and prevent other Visitors from coming in. When this happens, the door can stay locked for years. These are the worst times. Some Visitors return, eager to hear the man's tale once more, but by then the story has changed in their eyes and the man cannot remember the details that so enraptured them. When this happens, some Visitors grow angry and shut the door, never to return. Others find that they like the changes, because they themselves have changed.

The man knows nothing of the outside world because the room is his entire world. He spends his days inside its paper-thin walls, waiting for the door to open. He does not eat and he does not sleep, though perhaps it could be said that he dreams. His story, after all, must come from somewhere. It is unclear how old he is or how long the room has existed. He only knows that he himself has always been there, and thus it follows that the room must have always been there too.

    What the man does not know is that he is not alone. He is, in fact, one of many like him, hundreds of thousands of men in rooms much like his. Lined up side-by-side, stacked in formation like cells on a prison block, the rooms call to Visitors, beckoning them to open their doors. A man can be found behind each door, waiting. Like him they receive Visitors, like him they ramble on; endlessly, desperately, until someone props open the door, until somebody listens, until somebody stays.

(1, 169)

He Was Always Hers
C. Maris Bounds

Jack fiddled with the gold ring in his pocket as Mary did the dishes. She was humming softly in the peaceful evening, one of the first since her father had died on the beaches of Normandy a few months earlier. Jack took a deep breath.

'I got drafted, and I want you to marry me before I go.'

At the word 'drafted,' Mary stilled, sudsy plate in hand. Jack figured she hadn't heard anything after that. If she were anyone else, he figured she might've burst into tears – most girls he knew cried when their fellas got drafted. But Jack Bradford had known Mary Stevens for ten years, and she wasn't the kind to cry. Besides, he wasn't her fella, and she wasn't his girl.

—

In the summer of 1935, when Jack was twelve, he decided he never wanted to live another day without the scrawny little spitfire Mary Stevens. He and the other boys on their Brooklyn block were reenacting the fight between James J. Braddock and Max Baer from the radio. After getting pushed out of the ring of boys, Jack accidentally smacked the newly moved in Mary in the jaw, and she gave him a black eye before he could even say 'sorry.'

From then on, it was Jack and Mary or nothing.

At thirteen, Jack decided Mary was the girl he was going to marry. She was the only girl that seemed to get him. She defended him when he got roughed up and talked him down when his head got too big. Apparently, watching Mary scold him on the stoop of their building was quite the show. She was also the only one who didn't laugh at his dream of being a painter when he showed her his sketches of their classmates.

At fourteen, Jack decided being a painter wasn't going to be enough. His pops said he needed to start thinking about a real job if he wanted to make money. He wanted to marry her right out of school and live in one of those fancy apartments in Manhattan they'd seen in the magazines. He'd need money for that, so he had to do something else. Mary still gave him art supplies for his birthday and proudly hung the watercolor portrait he'd done of her in her room.

At fifteen, Jack caught Mary pushed up against the wall in the alley by their apartment, kissing Peter McDonald. He'd punched the snot-nosed brat. Before he could ask if Mary was okay, she slapped him across the jaw and refused to talk to him for two weeks. Those two weeks had been hell. But she forgave him eventually.

At sixteen, Jack decided to draw a line he'd never cross with Mary. He'd toe it with other girls, sure, but never Mary. She must have created a line long before he did because she never once crossed it with him. She never crossed it with others either. At least, she never said and none of the fellas in class boasted about it to him. Peter McDonald was a good enough reason to not boast to Jack about anything they might have done with Mary.

At seventeen, Jack decided Mary was always going to be the most important girl in his life, even if she'd never be his girl. He'd always remember the night when Mary's father dropped her off at Jack's family's apartment. He had wanted to get stupid drunk and didn't Mary to be alone. Jack remembered how she crawled into his bed and burrowed into his chest, whispering that her mom was gone. Killed in a car accident. He'd held her in his arms, promising that everything was going to be okay.

They kissed for the first time then. The only time.

It was panicked and greedy and painful. They stopped before it went too far. Mary pulled away and began sobbing. Right then, she just needed him to hold her. So, he did. They never talked about it again.

At eighteen, Jack decided to drop out of school to stay in New York, while his parents moved further West. He decided not to date. Girls liked him well enough. They flirted with him when he was drinking with the boys from the factory. When he flirted back, he told them he didn't want anything serious. Some told him they wanted more, others thought it was just fine. Mary never asked him where he'd been all night on the occasions she would head out to school and find him asleep outside his apartment door next to hers. If she noticed the lipstick on his collar or the red mark on his neck, she never mentioned them.

In the winter of that year, Roosevelt announced the United States was at war with the Japanese Empire.

At nineteen, Jack decided Mary and her father might be the only people in the entire world who believed in him. Mary had submitted one of the drawings he'd done of her father to the local paper for a contest. He'd won fifty dollars.

He took Mary out dancing. She smiled and told him how proud she was of him. Jack was going to tell her the same when a girl he'd once brought to his apartment asked to cut in and Mary let her. She slipped out of his grasp before he could even say she was the only one he ever wanted to dance with.

Sometimes Jack wished he could go back to when they were twelve and things weren't complicated.

At twenty, Jack decided he wouldn't go around with girls anymore.

Mary didn't ask him why he was suddenly free on Friday nights when her father asked him to come to dinner. Jack didn't ask why she hadn't found a guy either. When Mary's father was shipped off to Britain, Jack promised he'd look after Mary and held her hand as they watched her father's ship fade into the horizon.

At twenty-one, Jack was there when they got the letter about Mary's father in Normandy. He carried her to bed as she began to break into a million pieces, a muffled sob tearing against his chest as she pressed herself against him. Jack was all she had left.

He promised he would never leave her.

At twenty-one, Jack got drafted. –

He was afraid.

Afraid of leaving Mary alone in the city when she only had one year left to finish her degree. Afraid of going to fight in a war that never seemed to end, that swallowed boys whole, only to spit them out occasionally with missing limbs and addled brains.

He was afraid he'd be swallowed too.

He hated how he had no way out of it. He hated that he had no choice.

'Mary.'

She still wasn't looking at him. He stood up from the table and went to where she was standing by the sink, torn between what he needed and wanted to do. 'I want you to marry me before I go so you'll get my pension if . . . if . . .'

She was weeping, shoulders trembling at the sink.

He wasn't ready for Mary to cry as if he was already dead.

He wasn't ready for her to throw her arms around his neck and pull him into a kiss that tasted so much like a goodbye he started to cry too. He wasn't ready to lose her. He wasn't ready for the days he would have to live without wonderful, perfect, Mary Stevens.

Jack kissed her, tasting the salt of her tears. He picked her up and carried her to his bed. Mary clung to him and pulled at him as they desperately tried to be as close to one another as possible. He didn't want it to be like this. He didn't want their first time to be like this.

Instead, he buried himself in her arms as she wrapped herself around him.

He prayed this wouldn't be the end. He prayed they'd have a chance after it was all over. He prayed he would make it.

'I love you, Mary,' he breathed against her neck.

'I've always . . . always.'

'Come back to me, Jack,' she whispered, nuzzling a kiss to his temple. 'Promise me.'

He could see their future. They'd move into his apartment. His pops would walk her down the aisle. She'd wear one of her mom's old white dresses. He'd buy her a bouquet of red roses when she graduated from college. They'd name their kids after her folks. They'd get in fights over stupid things and make up because that's what they always did. They'd grow old together because that's all he'd ever wanted since he was twelve.

'I love you.' Jack slipped the gold ring around her finger.

Neighbourly Compassion
Sophie Lay

To my dear neighbours,

We are fortunate to be living so close to Lochrin Basin. How lucky we are that the rush and twist of the canal that traverses through the city terminates outside our apartment building. And what a pretty canal it is, with the water, gleaming silver under grey skies, populated by colourful boats moored up along its walls. And I like the quiet here, where the water slows down and laps against our courtyard while the city moves on around us. We're in the watchtower of the panopticon. Here, the windows face one another around the courtyard, and we use that to our advantage, don't we? From the third floor, when I sit in my armchair and turn off the lights, I can see you, Mr and Mrs Simmons, on the ground floor: watch as you sit down around your six-seater dining table. I can see you too, Isabel, on the fifth floor, your lights burning as you style your hair. Mostly, I see you, Andre Tate, opposite me, trying to feed your darling twins their dinner before it gets cold.

I am very careful with this vantage point and only use it to help you. I spotted the young woman attempting to climb through the window of the Simmons' flat two years ago, remember? If I hadn't called the police, she would have robbed us all.

But enough pleasantries. Let's talk about the elephant in the room.

I saw the men moored up on the canal just before Halloween, in that dark green houseboat. The peeling paint and mottled brass finishings stuck out among the much classier vessels. I first saw it when I took Midge out for her evening walk. I'm sure you all saw them; of course, you know how rude these men were. The voices inside were raucous. The windows were covered with lewd condensation.

I didn't realise that they were hedonistic creatures of the night at first so you couldn't be blamed for missing it either. They rose at six each evening, and their voices echoed around the canal. The noise upset Midge too, who took to hiding under my bed covers whenever the sounds arose. It kept me awake, so I spent my time watching. Even when I squinted, I struggled to make out their faces in the dark. They lit no bulbs on that boat and hid away from the beams of street lamps, distinguished only by their lit cigarettes, burning endlessly like hell's embers.

It was antisocial behaviour; there's no avoiding that. I couldn't have been the only one disturbed by it. Isabel, your lights burned all night, and Andre, I saw you up and down your hallway all night to comfort the twins. So I took the high road; I left a polite post-it note stuck to the window of their boat as I walked Midge in the morning: *This is a family neighbourhood. Please keep the volume down at night. Thank you!*

The following evening, the ruckus started up again in earnest.

This is not what polite citizens do to one another, and this is not the kind of behaviour we pay premium rents for. I do not object to people being out on their canal boats and throwing little parties down there. Plenty of people do this throughout the summer, and I have never had any objection before. But these men were having parties every single night without fail.

And, most importantly: they hurt Midge. My little darling, while out for a walk along the canal that snowy Saturday morning, found a marijuana cigarette on the pavement. There wasn't much of it left, but she's a small dog, a dear little Pomeranian. And those men, recklessly leaving their illegal drugs lying around, caused her harm. What if it had been your cat that had found it, Isabel? What if, Mr Tate, it had been one of your children?

Midge was half-dazed and completely out of her precious little mind. I felt helpless, clutching at her leash and watching her stumbling about in the snow like a drunkard. She couldn't walk straight and fell nose-first into the snow bank beside the footpath. I hope you can understand this, the fragility of her tiny trembling frame as I carried her to the veterinarian. It was cold. I was scared I'd left her out in it for too long. I thought it was my fault.

Then the veterinarian told me what she'd ingested. The fault lies with the men on the boat and the illegal drugs that they brought to our upright, family-friendly neighbourhood.

Retrospectively, at this point, we should have gone to the police. The men had no respect for my polite request and refused to come out when I knocked on their misty windows. The next logical step would have been to get the authorities involved. None of us took that step, and we all share the culpability for that lapse in judgement. And this, my dear neighbours, is why I'm writing to you.

I'm not saying that whoever took matters into their own hands was justified. But are these not the actions of a people's champion? Was it not simply a rogue hero enacting utilitarian justice? One could say that the men suffered, but don't forget that we suffered too: suffered sleepless nights and injured pets and the soiling of our peaceful haven of a neighbourhood. And we, remember, so greatly outnumber them.

And really, if one will insist on living on a canal boat through February, shouldn't one expect the cold? Or be prepared to be cast adrift? Even a child would know not to attempt to walk ashore across frozen waters – that's pure common sense. To call this mess 'manslaughter' is a gross inflation of the situation, however unfortunate it may be. I only pray that the poor man can rest in peace.

I bring you, therefore, to my point. We are more than just an apartment building or a neighbourhood. We are a community of like-minded individuals. We have been acting as a neighbourhood watch to one another for years now. I babysit your children, Andre. I keep a spare key for you, Mr and Mrs Simmons. Was it not I who stopped the burglar?

None of us, insofar as I'm aware, saw the culprit unlatch that rope, but we are all under the investigator's eye regardless. None among us is guilty of a crime – not that untying a rope should be considered one. We are all innocent, and we should not be turning our backs on one another at a time like this.

After all, we were together when we found him, huddled up on the dock steps like a piece of deformed scrap metal. The Tates were leaving for a school run; I was out walking Midge; Isabel was returning home. When I approached, the men on the boat were shouting to Mr Tate. They were stranded, frozen in the solid depths with sheets of ice stretching ten feet on either side. Between us and them, only three feet from the shore, a chasm had sunk through the ice layer. Murky waters lapped at the frozen lip of ice as Andre tried to talk to communicate with the man curled over on the dock steps, and the survivors on the boat. I rang the police. We were trying to help like upstanding citizens.

I took Midge inside and brought down blankets to throw out to those still stranded – two for the man who tried to swim ashore, who sat huddled in a ball, his lips cracked and his eyelashes frozen. We did everything in our power. I even took your daughters inside, Andre, while you dealt with the paramedics. I fed them hot chocolate and carrot cake until the terror ceased.

I do hope that they're feeling better, Andre.

It's for their sake, if nothing else, that we should come together. Amongst friends, like ourselves, there is no need to point fingers or draw conclusions, and certainly no need to whisper accusatory words into the ears of the detectives. We're all civilised people here; let's behave as such.

In this respect, I ask but a few favours from you all. Please do not be tempted to mention my visit to the veterinarians with Midge; it is such a trivial detail that could be blown out of proportion. Let's not stoop to such a level.

After all, I never chose to mention how you, Isabel, stood lamely aside while Andre and I attempted to assist the men on the boat. Not to mention, Mr and Mrs Simmons, how I've never reported *those* plants growing in the misty windows of your kitchen.

I only hope now that we can close this unfortunate chapter in our community with some grace and decorum. I greatly look forward to seeing you all soon.

With neighbourly compassion,

Ms Lucille Anne Washington.

Fear of Missing Out
Natasha Grodzinski

Are you living your life to its fullest potential?

Why not?

With Cermal Anti-Anxiety Medication, you have no excuse!

Take Cermal, and join the revolution saving a generation!

Get rid of those ugly and heavy feelings for good!

The ad ends and the dance music blaring from my phone's shitty speaker picks up again. I bop my hips, side to side. I spray perfume onto my neck.

I'm feeling bright and beautiful, and I'm going out tonight. Again.

I haven't spent an evening at home in months. The calendar plastered to the wall of my room proves it. The days passed coloured with large red checks.

I like people to see the calendar when they come over, so they can see how social I am.

See what a good User I am.

I catch my own eyes in the mirror and see dark bags underneath them. For a moment, it reminds me of how I looked when I was still controlled by anxiety. Before I became a User.

Speaking of.

I pop another pill for reassurance, what has now become a ritual whenever the ugly and heavy tries to worm its way back into my mind. I ignore the pile of books on my desk.

Coursework gets done in the morning. Sleep is for the dead.

That's from another Cermal ad, one of at least a dozen. Every half hour, one plays from my phone.

Haven't you ever wanted to do it all?

To not be limited by your own mind, or your own ugly and heavy feelings?

With Cermal you can!

Sleep is for the dead, and Cermal is for the living!

I remember mum, the last time I saw her, face twisted into an ugly and heavy expression.

'Sweetie, I know you've been having a tough time with your anxiety lately. But I really think you should consider going back to Doctor Barnes, not taking this . . .

whatever this drug is. I mean, who even are these people?'

I didn't bother to explain it, already knowing she wouldn't understand. It's not a drug.

Mental enhancer.

That's what they said to me over a year ago, when I passed by their booth on campus.

Something new. Something the world has never seen before. Something to combat the epidemic of anxiety and depression facing a generation.

It makes you focus when you want it to make you focus, makes you happy when you want to be happy.

A free six-month trial for students.

There was a woman there. A therapist. She said something like, 'All of the tools are inside your brain already; they're just not being used correctly. We can help you.'

I dab more concealer under my eyes and finally leave my apartment.

To Anna's, to pick her up.

As I walk, I see them. Flocks of them. Heading towards the City.

Somehow, you can always tell when someone is a

User. They look brighter and more beautiful than everyone else. They look happy. They look untouchable.

We all nod at each other as we pass. Some wave and some, clearly in the middle of a High, sprint over to me from the other side of the street. They sweep me into a hug. They tell me about a new bar that just opened in the City. It's massive. The best one this month. I should meet them there. We should all be friends. I say yes, excited, but I'm not on the same level they are. I'm jealous of their High.

I take another Cermal. Just in case.

I'm at Anna's door, a tall run-down house in a sea of tall run-down houses, and I can finally feel the early stirrings of a High. It's there in my gut, at the back of the neck, behind my eyes. That bright, beautiful feeling. Relief. I smile to myself. Then laugh.

I want to feel happy so I'm going to feel happy.

But that High, as soon as it becomes bright, a pleasant fire in my body.

It burns out.

I stop in her doorway.

In the same way you can always tell when someone is a User you can always tell when someone is a non-User.

I see Anna, and I know.

'What the fuck? When did you stop?'

'We stopped. Together.' She's talking about her boyfriend. He stands next to her like a bodyguard. Like he's expecting me to hurt her. Like he thinks they're better than me.

Non-Users.

I feel. Betrayed.

'Did *he* make you?'

She answers me by asking another question. That's something people do when they believe they're right, and the person they're talking to is wrong. 'Do you know what those drugs are doing to you?'

The bright feeling in my gut is ugly and heavy now.

'They're making me better.'

'They're making you worse.'

'We know someone who had a heart attack.' The boyfriend is talking. Motherfucker. 'She took too many and she died. She became addicted to them, but her depression got worse. Worse than before she started taking Cermal. They think they've got everyone under control but – '

He's interrupted by an ad that starts on our phones.

Haven't you ever wanted to do it all?

To not be limited by your own mind, or your own ugly and heavy feelings?

'Don't you see?' Anna again. 'You need to stop taking it, too. Once you do, you'll – '

I explode.

I start screaming. I tell her to shut up. She doesn't know what she's talking about. She's only saying this because of her boyfriend. He's feeding her Pro-Anxiety bullshit. She tries to talk, but I keep yelling over her. She comes near me, reaches for my hand. She sees my Cermals in my pocket and tries to take them.

I shove her away, and she falls. The boyfriend lunges for me. For my Cermals.

I run from the apartment.

I can feel my heart heaving in my chest. My lungs burning. My eyes wet.

No no no no no. This isn't what I was supposed to feel.

I take another Cermal.

Another.

Another.

My throat is dry, and they go down like rocks.

I want to feel happy, so I'm going to feel happy.

I run all the way to the City. I try to find that club those other Users mentioned, but on the way I find another group, just as High.

They offer me a Cermal with a shot of whiskey, and I take both.

And I don't know if we're in the club those others talked about, but it doesn't matter. Someone in the group hugs me and says we should be friends. I say aren't we already?

We're dancing somewhere dark and hot. There are people everywhere. No. Not just people. There are Users everywhere.

And then I think how happy I am. I think how perfect the moment feels when the song changes to something older, a classic, and everyone cheers.

I've now lost the group I came in with, but it's okay. I found a new one. New friends.

I do my best to take it in, the way you always have to. I take a video on my phone and share it. I want Anna to see it. Want her to see how Cermal makes everything better. Every moment is the greatest moment of my life.

But the thought suddenly makes me feel. Nervous.

What if this isn't the way life should be?

I stop dancing. No one notices.

That's the way I used to think. Before.

My vision swims.

And I feel. Anxious.

I dig into my pocket, but there are no Cermals.

Fuck.

But. Public bathrooms. They always have vending machines. I have my credit card.

I stumble there in the darkness. There is no High feeling in my gut anymore. Just a churning pool of ugly and heavy.

A User does not have ugly and heavy feelings.

I vomit into the first sink I come across.

The puke is bright yellow. Bile. It sticks to my hair.

The light in the bathroom is bright and harsh, broken up by the neon glow of the vending machine. A headache erupts behind my eyes.

This is because of Anna. She poisoned me with her own ugly and heavy feelings. She doesn't want me to feel bright and beautiful.

What do they know, non-Users? They don't get what it's like.

To feel the High after feeling the ugly and heavy for so long.

I want to feel happy, so it makes me feel happy.

I spit into the sink. I wipe my mouth with my hand. I meet my own eyes in the mirror.

There is yellow puke in my hair and shadows under my eyes and tiny red veins bursting out of their whites.

I look.

Not bright or beautiful.

Not like a User.

My phone sits on the counter. It lights up.

Are you living your life to its fullest potential?

Will of the Wisp
Issa Dioume

(Summer vacation rolled in, and with it came time for old friends to gather after many years . . .)

STREAMS POUR OUT Bouguenais Airport. His head – a round freckled mound – sails high above the rush of new arrivals. Elbowed towards the exit, left there looking stranded, he waits for waves to recede, then steps off the kerb and into the street.

Fumes rise off the melting asphalt. A jumble of flyers and newspapers scuttle beneath a row of broken lamps. Cars dot the parking lot in gold reflections. Every five minutes, whooshing along, buses empty or fill before heading into town.

Kedo's eyes sweep over cars with the bewildered air of a lost child, exposing his non-belonging – non-belonging to the fresh, vivifying air, homeward bound multitudes, and dirt-mottled clothes of the countryside crowd. Soon, he spots them.

Raymond's car idles ten-row's distance from the exit. Its crimson tint – dyed like childhood memories – and the two men lurking within give it away. Kedo enters the front passenger door, blowing his nose on a mauve pocket handkerchief. The smell of naphthalene seeps from his brown leather coat. A city-smell.

'So, I'm last to arrive, eh?'

'Indeed-indeed, city-boy!' exclaims Nandayo. 'Our ol' gang, finally reunited!'

'For the most part at least . . . ' notes Raymond, under his breath.

Nandayo sits splayed across the back seats, arms stretching sideways, clutching the outer seat-tops. He sports horn-rimmed sunglasses and a silk Hawaiian shirt. Glowing, a cigarette hangs between his two chapped lips.

'I bought us treats!' cries Raymond from the driver's seat. Long, black hair topples onto his shoulders – framing his face. His pale outstretched hand opens, revealing toffees in tinsel-blue, candy wrappers.

Both grab four apiece.

'Ready? Okay, *andiamo*!' he exclaims. 'Off to visit Kimyo.'

—

THIRTY-MINUTES LATER, the car glides down sinuous forest roads raising heaps of dust in its wake that powder sunken leaves in the verges. Clouds swirl aloft, swelling as it begins to rain. Far off into the horizon, a rainbow takes shape.

'Okay. So . . . we're lost, aren't we?' asks Kedo.

'Pfft! Isn't this your hometown?'

'It's yours too, Nandayo,' remarks Raymond.

'*Used* to be ours, *still* is yours!'

'We're lost right?'

'Yes . . . yes,' Raymond sighs. 'We're lost, Kedo. Not my fault, always struggled to find my way round these sticks.'

'I blame you,' says Nandayo.

'Why, thanks.'

'Think Kimyo will have whipped up a meal?' Raymond asks.

'Likely,' replies Kedo. 'Although, I wonder, why choose to invite us after all this time?'

Nandayo, acting uninterested, changes the subject. 'So uhm, Ray, roads seem like they've not changed one single bit inna decade, huh?'

'I s'pose.'

'And here we are! Back where everything started!'

'What?'

'C'mon Ray, don'tcha remember that tree?'

'What?'

Raymond eyes Nandayo. Then, following his pointed finger, he sees and remembers.

'Of course! We played round here. Our climbing tree'

'Exactly right.' Kedo nods. 'Furthermore, we passed by it already – precisely ten minutes ago.'

Raymond, scowling, says nothing.

'Might we be going in circles?'

He throws glances left and right in response.

Nandayo bursts out laughing.

'Shaddup Nanda!'

Kedo, now gazing out the window with head cupped in his palm, turns to them. 'Guys, stop. Nandayo, he's right. Shaddup. But Ray, stay civil okay? Don't get angry simply because city-boy over here,' he points to himself, 'is perceptive.' Without expecting an answer, he shifts back to the window.

More time passes. Branches loom above the road. Their leaves rustle with every wind sweep, casting flailing shadows over the car.

'Damn trees! Can barely see anything!' grumbles Nandayo. They whisk by a house; run-down, haggard and crippled. 'Wait, isn't . . . wasn't that . . . Maigo's old house?'

'Definitely,' confirms Kedo. 'When'd it get so . . . so dilapidated?'

'Began 'bout seven-years ago, when Maigo's mother remarried and moved to Paris,' says Raymond.

'That much time, eh? By the way, how long has it been since you two last saw Kimyo?' asks Kedo.

Raymond's fingers dribble nervously over the wheel. 'Hmm, no clue.'

'Been awhile,' Nandayo pauses. 'Round . . . twelve years, perhaps? Since . . . y'know, Maigo.'

'Yeah.'

Nandayo looks up, smoking a freshly lit cigarette. 'Well, after it happened, we went to different high schools and, kinda drifted apart.'

'Guess so. But you return every year for Bastille Day, and you,' he points a finger, 'you *live* here Ray. Why not visit Kimyo?'

'Mmmh, it's-like, y'know?' begins Raymond. 'I mean look at us. We've not met in years either, yet Nandayo still annoys the heck outta us. Childhood friends stay the same.'

'Ha-ha-ha! Yeah, I do, don't I,' Nandayo agrees.

'But still, isn't it strange? Kimyo inviting us out of the blue, after all these years. After what we did.'

'Maybe. Or, maybe it's just enough time's passed,' offers Raymond.

As if by an unspoken mutual agreement, a quietness establishes itself.

'Damn trees!' grunts Nandayo.

Overhead, branches web the sky. It gradually gets blotted out altogether. Then, a disconcerted look creeps onto Raymond's face, the look a man wears when regarding a source of profound unease. He points out into the murky penumbra.

'Mn-Mnemosyne River . . . we-we've come all the way out here?'

Dread squeezes their throats dry. At length however, Kedo speaks – releasing them from the clutches of silence as he wrestles out words.

'Any of you still mull over what happened that day?'

'No,' answer the two, somewhat feebly.

'Oh. I do.'

They look around, nervous. Desperate to break the tension, Nandayo mocks Kedo. 'Oh-Ooooh. Dost anyone ruminate over bygone days . . . I profoundly wonder.'

Nobody laughs.

'Ha-ha,' retorts Kedo, tartly. 'But, at the crux of the matter – '

'At the crux of the matter? By golly! How two years in Paris have occasioned most pedantic a change!'

'Whatever.'

'Nanda, I already said shu – ' Raymond cuts in. 'Wait, what's happening?'

The car teeters and sways uncannily.

'I can't steer!' he exclaims. 'The wheel, it – it – it's . . . stuck!'

As though gifted with a mind of its own, the car swivels right, left, right, then wills itself off the road and down a forest slope, somehow skimming around tree-trunks by a mere hair's breadth, before reaching a clearing where it stops abruptly, at Mnemosyne's bank.

They exit to check for potential damage to the car. Frosted cogongrass crunches underfoot, and breath forms into white tufts which dissolve in the enveloping mist. The crisp, cold, air stings their cheeks red. It is dark. Nandayo's hands go numb.

'Hey, how long've we been driving?'

'Dunno . . . an hour at most. Why?' Raymond still seems dazed from the car's bizarre defiance.

'Look!'

With tree branches no longer cloaking it, the sky comes into full view, now wearing night's starry coat. Everything but the night sky is concealed by the murky mist, which hangs heavily.

'Wha – How?'

The river – an icebound mirror – is rock-solid. Suddenly, a bell rings and a tiny figure congeals into form in the mist. No. It is the mist. Silver-skinned and carrying a crosshatched lantern, it flies over the river and settles on a bridge. Illuminated, scribblings carved upon a supporting pillar reveal themselves: '*Le Pont De Biais.*' The figure seems familiar to them.

'Is that – ?' starts Nandayo.

'Maigo?' finishes Kedo, shocked.

'But, he – he – he drowned here.'

'Hey? Wasn't this bridge destroyed after they opened the dams?' asks Raymond.

Yet there it stood. A completely unbroken, undeniable, sturdy bridge of wood; thirty-feet wide and two storeys high.

The figure stirs, revealing yet another engraved

pillar which reads: 'FIND OUT.'

Then, it leaps onto the railing and walks, balancing masterfully like a funambulist. Unexpectedly, however, another figure appears. It is shadowy, its head tilts slightly to one side. It rushes out and shoves Maigo's figure off the bridge. As he falls, cracking the ice, he disappears and so too do the shadowy figure and the bridge.

Sun and warmth return, as if all had been an illusion.

'What the hell? Was that Maigo?' asks Nandayo.

Kedo rubs his chin. 'Yes, I think. Maybe, in spirit or something. Perhaps he was why the car acted as it did. Did he mean to bring us here?'

'But, what was that . . . that other thing?' wonders Raymond.

'I don't know. Why'd Maigo's spirit do this?'

'To remind us what happened.'

So after years of denial, they finally do it. They remember that day.

'When it happened, Kimyo was with Maigo, right?' asks Raymond.

'Yeah, my dad worked at the police station. I was there,' recalls Kedo. 'He came to report what'd happened, as the only witness of the "accident." Except, he was bruised, like someone who'd just fought.'

'Bruised? Ya sure?' asks Nandayo.

'Positive. Crying, too.'

They allow silence to occupy the air. Before Raymond chases it away.

'He was never the same after that,' he recalls. 'The reserved Kimyo we knew vanished. He was constantly happy after Maigo's death. As though it had released something in him. While us, we were sad of course – and angry.'

'That day, before it happened . . . I remember that they argued. And, they walked home together afterwards, since they were neighbours, and they took the path with the bridge. That's how Kimyo bore witness to Maigo's fall. At least, that's what the police said. But, was he just a witness?' wonders Kedo.

'Not just then,' Raymond notes. 'Always. Kimyo hated Maigo's relentless teasing. Told me so himself.'

'D'you think?'

'No – nah. Not enough to – C-could he have . . . killed Maigo?'

'Out of annoyance, he might've snapped,' says Kedo.

'Really?' asks Nandayo. 'But then, why? With everything we did after Maigo's "accident," with how we ignored him – '

'We shouldn't have done that.'

'But maybe we knew, maybe somewhere, deep down, we just know,' Raymond manages. 'Isn't that why we all came? To confirm it?'

'Him inviting us after all this time. Is it remorse or .

. . '

'Only one way to know. '

Together, they heave the car back up the slope and onto the road. They clamber in and drive. Theories still flutter high in their heads. This time, nothing goes awry; Raymond drives the car, not the other way around. And, heavy-hearted, they finally arrive.

Kimyo stands by the doorway. He is overdressed for the occasion and wearing white nitrile gloves. His hands grasp a long, sharp, kitchen-knife. A peculiar smile sits on his lips, he tilts his head to the side and his bulging, staring eyes, wink awkwardly at them.

'I've been waiting.' His long fingers caress the shiny blade. 'Do come in gentlemen. Lunch, is served!'

(4, 194)

From the Ceiling
M.E. Gerretsen

Max often wondered what it would be like to live on the ceiling. He thought about it before going to sleep, as his mum read to him from *The Rainbow Fish,* and he thought about it in the few minutes between his one mum nudging him awake and the other saying that now he really, really had to get up or he'd be late for school again. The idea of escaping the conventional realm of his bedroom floor and rising into the air and landing with both feet on the ceiling seemed to him a much greater adventure than whatever mischief his classmates got up to. But then, they never invited him anyway.

That Friday morning, Max was ill. His mum Julie gave him a stern look and asked him if it was a real sickness or one of his pretend ones, and then she felt his forehead and took his temperature. On the high side, but only a little. She consulted with his mum Tabitha, who was running around gathering keys, phone, and packed lunch, rushing to get to work before the motorways were jam-packed. She built bridges for an engineering company, and Max thought that was the most impressive thing anyone could do. They observed him as he lay there, squeezing his plush dolphin in fear that he would be sent to school, but they allowed him to stay home, and he squeezed a little less.

His mum brought him honeyed tea and opened one of his curtains to let in some daylight, but not too much so he could still sleep if he wanted to. A cold winter's light crept in. Max didn't want to sleep, but he didn't want to get up and lie on the couch and watch daytime TV either. He decided today would be the perfect day for his trip to the ceiling.

The ascent was easy. It gave him the same pleasant feeling in his stomach that he got whenever his mum drove over a high bump without slowing down. When he landed he found the ceiling to be quite warm and he remembered his mum telling him how heat likes to find a high spot. He was in a landing position, arms stretched outwards for balance, when his shirttails fell over his head and the hem of his pyjama pants dropped to his knees. Max stood up straight and tucked in his shirt but found there was no solution for the pants; they kept falling up. He decided to let them and looked around.

He was standing in the middle of his ceiling near the light, a blue shade with Nemo fish on it, swimming upside-down. He walked towards it, carefully, like a crane on thin ice. A pleasant warmth radiated from the lamp, as well as a soft buzzing sound that he only heard now that he was close to it. A spider web had gathered where the canopy attached to the ceiling. Max chose this as a good spot to observe his surroundings, and sat down.

His furniture hung like bats in a cave. The foreignness of their new position was overwhelming at first but did not take long to get used to. Above him, in a bed that seemed too big, a boy of about seven years old was glued to the mattress, holding a plush dolphin as big as himself. Max waved at him, but floor-Max didn't seem to be aware of ceiling-Max's presence and kept staring down with a dreamy expression. There was a chair at the foot of the bed from which a collection of plush marine creatures looked down – a fluffy white seal with particular curiosity. In the centre of the room a steam train dangled from its tracks, as odd-sized clay animals held on to the carpet for dear life.

Max sat there for a while, enjoying his new perspective. He had always thought the ceiling to be a plain white but now that he was on it he noticed it was actually closer to egg-shell. Furniture he had always thought of as being upright made just as much sense hanging upside-down. Intrigued to discover more, Max began to explore further. He had never realized how high their ceilings were, until he found himself stretching for the door head and reaching high and jumping before he could pull himself up and climb through the door frame. With a *thump* he landed on the other side, in the long and narrow first-floor hallway.

To his left and right – the guestroom and his Mum's study respectively – he found the doors closed. Unable to open them from his high spot, he kept walking. The stairwell on his right was alarmingly high, a gaping cavity of ground floor. Then came the door leading to his mothers' bedroom, closed too. But the bathroom door in front of him was open.

The ventilation fan hummed on his left and the windows were still foggy from his Mum's shower and the whole room smelled like her arnica shower oil. Max grinned at seeing the toilet so high up and wondered if he could still hit his mark but he resisted the urge to try and instead stood looking into the shower cabin for a while. The top of the showerhead was the wet kind of dusty, one of those places that was often forgotten during the weekly cleaning. Max would have wiped it off now, had he been able to reach it. The showerhead, he decided, would have to remain in limbo. A hanging plant in a cane basket rose from the ceiling in the corner below the laundry basket and from Max's perspective it looked like a flame or one of those nymphs in a storybook with twigs for hair. He hauled it in to check if it had been recently watered, feeling like a deckhand on a pirate ship, except the content of this bucket was dry. Max made a mental note to tell his Mum.

He sat down near the ventilation fan. Its purring was oddly calming, like the cat they might have owned if Max hadn't been allergic. He lay down. Maybe he would take a nap. The bathroom was nice and warm, and the smell of arnica made him feel safe. Zoom said the fan.

Then he heard the soft footsteps of his Mum in her house slippers on the wooden stairs and he sat up and peeked out the bathroom door. She looked into his bedroom, found floor-Max fast asleep, and retreated to her study, coffee cup in hand. She left the door open, and ceiling-Max quietly followed her in.

She sat down behind her book-covered desk. She was translating another one, Max knew, but from up high all words looked the same to him. He sat down right above her to watch her work. He liked the idea of life continuing with him so far away from it, like being in the backseat of his Mums' car and looking out the window and not needing to do anything. The smell of arnica had followed them in. Max could only hope the coffee in its mug would abide by the laws of gravity and remembered that time when he was three years old and had knocked his Mum's coffee cup off the table and was taken to the hospital with second degree burns. He hadn't seen her drink coffee for some time after that. Now coffee was back, but under constant supervision whenever Max was near.

The phone rang. She let it do so for a while before picking up, as was her habit.

'Hello?'

The muffled voice on the other side didn't carry to the ceiling.

'Yes, he is at home. I called earlier.'

The voice muffled on.

'No, he's ill. I told your secretary.'

Both ceiling-Max and floor-Max shifted uncomfortably.

'What makes you say that?'

Her tone changed.

'He's never mentioned that to us.'

The muffling continued for a while. A sound not unlike the buzzing of the lamp or the purring of the bathroom fan but with none of their charm.

'I don't think it's for you to decide what he should be embarrassed by or not.'

There was a sharpness to her voice that pulled Max back into reality, and a heaviness like an anvil shackled to his stomach dragged him down. He retreated to his bedroom so that when he fell he would land in his bed and not on the floor, and once there he let reality take him. The descent was like the landing of an airplane or falling in a dream: fast and hard-hitting upon touch-down. He wished he could have stayed on the ceiling. He wished everyone would live on the ceiling, where everything was different and that was just the way it was, but the ceiling couldn't shield him.

He left the comfort of his bed and his imagination and made his way to his Mum's study where she sat frowning still holding the phone. She smiled when she saw him enter.

'Hi gup, how are you feeling?'

He hugged her in silence, but she seemed to understand.

Of Relative Colours
Angelo Castiglioni

As a small child, I was fascinated by my father's constant painting – though I had no notion of what it was really about. I spent hours watching him put layer upon layer, mixing paints and with broad strokes spreading them across the canvas. The colours were frightening and bold, giving me the impression – although I lacked the vocabulary to express it at that age – that he was illustrating life by capturing it the way he chose to imagine it. As I grew up, I became more aware of the world and noticed that every day my father painted the same picture over again. The paintings both confused and scared me. They were all simultaneously a portrait, a landscape, a still life, a motion, and some sort of edifice all at once. It wasn't until I was much older that I came to understand what he sought to achieve. It wasn't until I was old that I was able to perceive the nature of his quickening campaign.

—

When I was eight, I asked him, for the first time, what he was painting. He answered me with a story. 'This painting is of the time my friends and I sailed for Morocco,' he started. 'Neither my companions nor I had ever sailed open waters before, never having even left the marina. But we were determined and driven by the confidence of youth. Not a week out, a savage squall descended upon us and tore our mainsail. Fortunately – for I did not know how to swim – we had a most righteous ballast that kept us upright. After the storm died we slept, using the small motor to keep us moving. When the gas ran out, we smoked cigarettes, hoping the currents would carry us to land. Some days later, we drifted into view of an island, which I learned was called São Miguel. It was marvellously pigmented; massive emerald cliffs speckled in ruddy flowers that descended into the sea like a fragment of Pangaea broken away and preserved in all its majesty. Of course, humans lived there too, and to our great relief they spotted us and pulled us into harbour. The town of Ponta Delgada exploded with rich vivacity. Though we spoke no Portuguese, they welcomed us like we were their children. Nights were kaleidoscopes of tumbling shapes and sounds; days were gardens of serenity. Being seafaring people, they happily fixed our sails in exchange for some light labour and song.' My father sat back and grinned at his wild recklessness. 'We never reached Morocco. After staying on the island several weeks, we sailed home with renewed potency.'

I didn't know where this island was or what it represented, but his enthusiasm gave me extravagant dreams.

—

At fifteen, I remember asking about the painting again while sitting in the living room listening to Zeppelin records. I must have asked on numerous occasions before that, but this moment remains vivid. 'This painting is of the time I went to the Amazon in search of the Lost City,' he explained. I was unaware he had ever been to South America. I was already far less interested in explorers as I was in rock 'n' roll, but his story held my attention. 'Two of my friends and I bet a man from Harvard we could find what Percy Fawcett had failed to discover in 1925. Our strategy was to start in Colombia and work our way inland, instead of starting in Rio as others had done. In truth, we had little knowledge of any previous expeditions and had only heard of Fawcett from a drinking game we used to play with the encyclopaedia. But the drunkenness of our souls lasted well past our hangovers. Suffice to say, we landed in Bogotá with very little to go on but that the Amazon was southeast, that it was a vicious green beast full of warriors and demons. Crossing into Brazil, we were stopped by paramilitary who claimed to be guerilla communists. Our presence there did not please them. When it became clear to them we did not even know where "there" was, they sent us home alive.' My father's voice faltered on that last sentence. He said no more. He had always appeared to me as somewhat square; the idea of him in the jungle seemed ludicrous.

—

When I was twenty-two, he still painted every day, and every day it was the same beautiful and terrifying scene. I visited after graduating from university; I asked him then what he was painting. 'This painting is of the time I crashed my motorcycle.' He did not smile. 'It was February and a grey winter and I had recently lost my first wife to cancer.' I didn't know he had a motorcycle, let alone a 'first wife.' 'I was on Highway one. For two years I lived with her in California in hopes of escaping the cold, but it found me there anyway. She was the first woman I ever loved. She defied life's transience. She crafted eternity by pursuing the beauty in each moment. Every minute, every word, she could extract their essence and revel in them forever. The week she died I wanted to be dead too. Lost, I spent an evening at the Fernwood Bar in Big Sur, mixing the spirits of the woods with the spirits of drink, hoping to find a curative cocktail. Around midnight, I went looking for Henry Miller. I crashed that night going eighty miles per hour. I can't remember if it was on purpose. It was only thanks to a dense mass of lilac bushes that caught me that you were born.' I cried when I left. I wondered if mom knew, and I was angry for her.

—

On Christmas, when I was twenty-nine, father was still painting the all too familiar depiction. Age had caught up with him, deepening the lines on his face. His mind seemed somewhat distant, detached. I was concerned. Hesitant, I asked what he was working on. 'This painting is of the time I published my book.' Growing up reading his articles, I knew him just as a journalist. It was a shock to hear he had published a book. I wondered if this was true. 'It was successful but sold exclusively in Europe. During the fifties, high-pitched-wordism collections with scarlet covers were not so well regarded in America, unless you were edgy like Salinger or Kerouac, but I was never so acutely hip. I wanted to turn rusted words sapphire, to show the hungry bones beneath. After a decent run overseas, however, people developed expectations of my next work; expectations I couldn't meet. I spent years searching, but disappointed my fans.' I wanted to know more about this book – if it existed. Before I could ask, mom called from the dining room that the turkey was ready. The evening passed quickly without further explanation. I forgot about the book soon after I left.

—

One spring when I was thirty-six, I brought my fiancée home to meet my parents. I already knew my father would be painting. His absurd repetition worried me. Mom assured me – as she then often did – that he was fine. I didn't ask about the image for fear of embarrassing him in front of his new daughter-in-law. I hadn't talked to her of the paintings. He proceeded to tell us anyway. 'This painting is of the time I met your mother.' The lightness in his voice was illuminated by the joy on his lips. 'She was a golden meteor that impacted my frozen planet; shattering it to stardust, only then set free to reform in the image of love, in the likeness of me but with the graces of her.' Before returning my attention to my fiancée, I remember being moved by his words. Moved, and frustrated. It was then I first recognised the shallowness in my own relationship.

—

At forty-three, divorced, career, two children, I saw my parents less. Father went to the ER. Arterial embolism before declining into dementia, which would plague him the next seven years. I visited the hospital to find him sitting in bed, with his paints, painting the same scene with the same violent and pointless colours. I was furious. I wanted to tear it apart. His stroke was finely measured. His words were disjointed. 'This paint is time born. Cadmium honey locust quakes in fall, of rhythms and immortality.' I was too angry to interpret his words. The days already moved so fast. After that, he couldn't remember my name.

—

Fifty. Funeral. Eighteen thousand three hundred and seven paintings. All the same, all different. An infinite vitality of relative colours. 'He started when you were born.' Mom knew every story. I wept the spectrum of his palette. Trying to reverse the acceleration of time. His will to me: easel, brushes, paints.

—

I now paint every day.

The Club
Julie Galante

Welcome, my dear! Come in, come in, have a seat. Can I get you some tea? Why don't I just get you some tea. My, you new girls get younger every year. Forty-two? My, that *is* young. Not the youngest we've ever had, no – not by decades – but certainly well below average. And he was your age? Yes, I figured you didn't look like a trophy wife.

Now, we'd better get started. Here's your handbook and welcome basket. I'd just like to go over a few key items with you, if you don't mind. First: little packs of tissues. I recommend carrying several of these everywhere you go – stick them in your handbag, the pockets of all your coats, everywhere. Also, some wipes for cleaning your eyeglasses. It's hard to see clearly through all those tear stains.

Next: paperwork. You'll need to get started on it right away. There will be so much paperwork. And some grief, too. But mostly paperwork. Death certificates, insurance forms, overseas call centres where they offer you their sincerest condolences before launching into a sales pitch for upgrading your plan. Death is considered a big sales opportunity these days.

I used to think all the paperwork was an unnecessary cruelty, but maybe it's just the world's way of keeping us amongst the living. Speaking of which – you'll quickly realise that it's tempting to hole up at home, but *do* try to get out. At least come here, to the clubhouse.

You'll find a t-shirt in your welcome basket that will identify you as a club member. You may find it helpful to wear this out in public for the first few weeks. It says WIDOW in big pink letters, isn't that nice? Some of the girls think it's a bit much, but *I* found it very helpful, indeed. We used to hand out veils – but they're so *old-fashioned*, and make some people think of terrorists these days. So we thought we'd better come up with something else: a new look for the Modern Widow.

It's a lot, I know. You must still be in shock. It's surreal, the way that the world just goes on. Your fingernails will keep growing. Not those of the deceased, that's a bit of nonsense, but yours, you, the surviving one. You'll wonder at their ability to carry on as if nothing has changed.

Then there's all the stuff. All his stuff. Don't try to get rid of it right away. Wait until those ratty old running socks and concert t-shirts start to feel like clutter, rather than reminders. The sentimentality will come off of some items with time. Not all, but some.

Some people will treat you like royalty. It will feel

undeserved, but do try to let yourself enjoy it. Let yourself enjoy anything you possibly can. Feel the relief of realising that you can still have fun. I know you don't believe me now, but you'll see.

Goodness, I've gotten off track! Okay, that's you all registered. Let's just go for a quick tour, shall we? Down this hallway we have the Prayer Room, the Meditation Room, and the Tai Chi Room. And that way is the Relaxation Oasis and the Therapy Room – we offer group sessions for members with particular *circumstances*. How did yours go? Leukaemia? I see. Well, at least you won't be needing the suicide support group.

Over here, we have the Grieving Rooms. They're soundproof and contain plenty of tissues. You can sign up for fifteen-minute sessions. We recommend going for the same time every day – helps to get your grief on a tight schedule.

Back in that corner is Sally the Matchmaker's office. You probably won't be visiting her anytime soon, but you never know. Some women are in there faster than the body's gone cold. Just can't bear the feeling of being alone. We call them the Revolvers. Best not bother getting to know them too well – they won't be around long enough to be worth your while.

And, that's us! Come hang out in the clubhouse whenever you like. You're free to come and go as you please, just be sure to show your membership card at the door. If there's anything else I can do for you, just ask. After all, our aim is to be the very best club you never wanted to join.

(2, 195)

Sparks
Aylssa Osiecki

Nora Brown was running. Not the strained, sweating through a rough cotton t-shirt running of gym class – this was different than any running she'd ever done in her life. She was a human laser, slicing along the roadside fast enough to pass cars moving in her direction. She could hear everything happening within her body in deafening high fidelity: heart pumping, blood sluicing through her veins, muscles twitching with precision as her arms and legs pumped in unison. She could feel each hair in her scalp trailing out behind her, every pore pumping sweat and sebum, even the distinct squish of a zit pushing itself up between dermis and epidermis.

gentle vibration beneath the top layer of her skin. It made a low, persistent hum that only she could hear, like the buzz of power lines on a hot July day. It was always in the background, like radio static.

    At first the hum seemed like just another uninvited thing that arrived at puberty, like boobs and armpit smell and the way suddenly her mom's voice asking her to do *anything* sounded like fingernails on a blackboard. Eventually Nora got used to it. Now she thought little of the way that papers seemed to fly off of desks and perfectly stable glasses of water toppled unprovoked in her presence. When her mom was in a good mood, she blamed it on puberty. 'Adolescence,' mom would cackle. 'It's like my daughter has some kind of force field around her.'

When mom was in a bad mood, the hum caused fights.

Nora felt the hum tingling in her fingertips on those afternoons when she came home from school, turned the key in the lock and knew before she even opened the door that mom would already be on the couch. The hum vibrated through her gut as she watched her mom lying there, looking as if she was drifting out to sea on a small raft and doing nothing, absolutely nothing to save herself.

She felt the hum rumble down to her toes the day they dropped Rory off at his special school.

'There'll be other kids like him there,' her mom said, with a smile that drooped like damp washing on the line. She knew Rory was different. He barely talked, he did everything in the same exact order every day, and he couldn't stand strangers and loud noises. Other kids had always called him mean names – but she'd done her best to stand up for him.

'Nora, it's not up to you to be his champion,' her mother said one day in a rare moment of lucidity. As they drove home without Rory, the hum rose in nauseating waves. What mom didn't understand was that Nora needed Rory too. He was her best friend. Around him the hum was gentle. She felt calm and in control.

When Nora felt nervous, the hum became an overwhelming throb in her skull. Sometimes it was powerful enough to momentarily break the seal between her thoughts and other people's. It seemed to get stronger when she was angry.

And today, the hum had knocked over more than just a glass of water. Today, the hum had broken through her; it had hurt somebody.

—

Nora hadn't woken up that morning intending to run away from school. The need came over her at morning recess while perched sentinel above the rest of the playground on the uneven bars. She knew she was too old to play on them (nobody else in eighth grade did) but she liked the vantage point being up high gave her.

She couldn't stand the idea of going back into school, not after what had happened in the girl's bathroom that morning. Nora thought of the thin rivulet of blood she'd seen pouring out of Meg Atkinson's nose and the knowledge that she had caused it. She thought of the look of panic on little Josie's face when she saw it too and knew that it was Nora's fault. Nora was usually the one locking herself in the bathroom stall with her feet propped up on the toilet until Meg and her friends receded to class.

Not today though.

Today they'd found Josie – a new 6th grader who'd cried on the first day of school – first, perched on a toilet seat with a pair of bloody underpants balled up in her hand. Meg stood above her, dangling a rough generic school sanitary pad just out of her reach.

'Say please like a big girl, Jo-Jo, and maybe we'll give it to you.' Meg said. The collective laughter of her and her friends was just low enough to avoid announcing their mischief to any nearby teachers. With Meg's attention trained on Josie, Nora could have slipped in and out of the bathroom cubicles unnoticed – if it weren't for the look she'd seen on Josie's face.

The look, coupled with the hum pulsating beneath her skin made Nora speak up. The hum vibrated in her throat as Meg turned and was surprised to hear Nora Brown speaking up, and that her voice sounded almost like a grown up's.

'What's the matter Nora? Do you need a pad too?' Meg asked. Nora could sense Meg was feeling a bit smaller than usual, and this feeling made the hum stronger.

'Nobody thinks you're funny, Meg. Just give her the pad and shut up.' Nora could feel something rumbling through Meg. Shame? The hum was ringing in her ears now, filling her up.

'And nobody cares what you think, Nora,' said Meg, grabbing up her confidence in frantic little fistfuls. 'Why don't you go back to being a loser and hanging out with your wino mom and your retarded little brother?'

For an instant, Nora flushed with embarrassment. The wino mother – that she couldn't defend. But *that word* Meg called Rory – Nora's insides fizzed with rage. She opened her mouth to say, 'He's not –' but instead, a crack opened in her. She felt the hum burst through her chest, she saw Meg flung back against the white tiled wall, her blue eyes wide with surprise. She saw the ribbon of blood escape Meg's nose.

'I definitely did that,' Nora thought.

Just how though, she wasn't sure.

Nora hadn't lifted a hand.

The air was taut. Nobody moved. The sanitary pad lay on the white tile floor in its protective wrapper. Nora picked it up and offered it to Josie. She was still seated on the toilet clutching her stained underwear. She shrank as Nora came closer. Josie snatched the pad from Nora's outstretched hand and yanked the cubicle door shut. Nora couldn't understand why. She'd just been trying to help.

Then the school bell clanged and Meg's friends filed soundlessly out of the bathroom, giving Nora a wide berth as they passed. Meg stood still against the bathroom wall, one finger dabbing at the blood trickling from her nose. Nora couldn't help feeling sorry for Meg for a moment. What good was having a posse of mindlessly loyal friends if they ditched you in a moment like this?

By reflex, Nora moved to grab her a tissue from the dispenser, to say sorry. But Meg's words vibrated in her ears again, and Nora decided that Meg did not need help from a loser girl with a wino mom and retarded little brother. She left the bathroom, joining the crowd of students who were streaming outside for morning recess.

—

The moments flickered behind Nora's eyes once more, like frames from a comic book. It had really happened. The hum was real, and other people could feel it too. This changed everything.

Nora filed out into the schoolyard. Around her, her classmates moved in the same little dramas that played themselves out in daily fifteen-minute increments. Nora was surrounded by hundreds of other students slapping basketballs against the asphalt, waving the remains of packed lunches in little plastic baggies, weaving between each other in perpetual games of tag that nobody ever seemed to win. She wondered if any of them could feel the hum too – and if they did, were they afraid of her like Meg and Josie were?

Nora gripped the metal of the uneven bars and felt it vibrate against her fingertips. This time she felt it reverberate in her brain too, a sickly-sweet bit of excitement that jarred her with its rightness. The hum filled her with confidence. It was decided. She was in charge now, she called the shots, and she wouldn't be hiding in bathroom cubicles anymore. She was going to see Rory.

Nora hopped down from the uneven bars. She crossed the playground, each footstep creating mini-earthquakes only she could feel. She strode toward the thicket behind the school, buoyant with her new power. Her heart rose, full as a helium balloon. And before she knew it, Nora Brown was running.

(5, 121)

In the Attic
Elena Sims

It's been twelve days since Dad went missing, but Mom still puts out his morning coffee.

She makes her way to the opposite end of the breakfast table and eases into the wicker chair, deflating with a sigh. Her hand is clenched into a fist on the table. Liver spots dot the top. I can't remember if they were there last time I visited.

Bringing a pink sugar packet to her lips, Mom tears it open and spills it into her mug. She then grabs a spoon and begins stirring. The radio wafts swing music from the kitchen counter around the corner.

'One of Dad's favorites,' she says.

'I remember,' I say, looking down at my phone.

I haven't been to work in over a week and wasn't sure how long I'd be gone. Dad always went on walks. It was normal. The doctors said he was still fine enough to go alone. I guess he walked too far this time and got lost.

Clicking my phone off, I catch my reflection in the dark screen. Black stubble sprouts along my jaw with purple bags nestling deep beneath my eyes. I scratch my chin and put my phone down.

Scraping comes from the ceiling above, accompanied by a series of thuds.

'The rats have been bad this week,' I say.

The house is old, raised on stilts over thick marshland and has always been prone to rats sneaking inside the plaster walls. My childhood was filled with the sound of tiny nails tapping vertically above my bed, as I imagined thousands of bodies piling atop each other, climbing into the attic.

We found an opossum in there once, when the ceiling thumps had gotten so bad Dad couldn't ignore them anymore. It was dead, fur damp and rancid, like soured milk.

Our flashlights glanced over the corpse as dozens of little eyes reflected back. The stomach was opened, mush spilling out onto the planks. A few rats that were still eating looked up at us. Their heads soaked like brush-tips dipped in red paint. They scattered to the shadows.

'Damn,' Dad said, then went back down for a garbage bag.

I waited there for him to return, my flashlight on the opossum.

Thuds sounded from all directions as they crawled into crevices, watching from the corners. I could feel them there, licking the blood from their fur and waiting for us to leave. Upset that we had come, that we had interrupted their feast.

Mom stirs her coffee as her clenched hand knocks a messy rhythm against the table. My phone rings. It's Jimmy.

'Hey buddy,' I say.

Jimmy is a friend from high school who joined the police after graduating. He called me two days after Dad had disappeared and told me the news. I was surprised Mom hadn't thought to call about Dad going out for a pack of cigarettes and never coming back.

Then again, I wasn't much for conversations, and I couldn't remember the last time Mom, and I had spoken on the phone. Probably when Dad started, 'falling into memories,' as Mom called it.

'He thinks he's back there,' she had said on the phone a few months ago.

I was pulling my suit jacket on, trying to find my keys. 'Just let him reminisce, there's no harm in it.'

'He keeps walking longer at night, Andy. He even mistook me for –'

Her voice cut off like she wouldn't allow herself the next word, but I knew. I knew without her needing to say it.

'Who would he mistake you for?' I asked anyway.

'You know *who,*' she whispered harshly, then hung up.

The rats are scraping hard against the ceiling above the breakfast table like they are yanking at something. Maybe another opossum. From the number of thuds gathering, it must be big.

'I'll get a bag and go up there in a bit,' I say.

'Oh, don't trouble yourself,' Mom says. 'The rats will take care of it eventually.'

Dad hadn't accounted for the rats when he built the house. Used to boast about making it for Mom right after Vietnam.

'She always wanted a house on the water,' he would murmur, eyes lost in the marsh.

I would listen as he pointed out the wood-storks fishing, mosquitoes hovering above the sawgrass, and the occasional alligator snout rising from the muck.

'This is the simple life I promised her,' he would say.

Dad was wrong. Mom had wanted to live in the suburbs, and she wasn't shy about it. But he never seemed to hear her when she said it. He would be too lost in the marsh by then, looking out, past the tall grass to where the mud changed into water and swept into the channel. It was in those moments, when his eyes drifted along the yellow fields, that I realized it wasn't Mom he saw out there.

'He only wanted to build the damn house when he got back,' Mom had said once after a bad fight between them.

I had caught her cutting him out of a picture. It showed men in matching green uniforms with greasy faces, their eyes staring at the camera. Except Dad's. His trailed off to something unseen, the only hint being a slender, pale hand in the corner of the frame. He was smiling so big I hadn't recognized him at first.

Mom snapped the scissors and Dad's head fluttered to the floor. 'This isn't my home.'

Jimmy tells me he hasn't found anything on Dad yet. Makes sense. Twelve days is a long time for a cigarette run.

'He hasn't found anything,' I say to Mom.

She nods, her clenched hand tightening, knuckles turning white.

It was easy for Mom to be angry at Dad. All she had to do was glimpse the handkerchief he carried around. A delicate white cloth, with MPT initialed on the bottom right corner. I had asked her about it once when she found it in his jean pocket while doing laundry.

'A gift from someone he met in Vietnam,' was all she said and dropped it into the washer.

When Dad found it later during dinner, the material had turned a patchy brown, the threaded initials running. He threw chairs, yelling she had done it on purpose. Mom shouted back, but I couldn't hear over the shattering of plates.

'Go back then!' she cried, flinging a gravy saucer.

The dish smashed against the wall, crumbling to the ground.

Frenzied scraping erupted from behind the plaster then as hundreds of feet rushed to the opposite side. We all stood in silence as the tiny thuds washed over us.

'The rats are back,' Dad said, straightening his chair and sitting down.

He stabbed his steak. Mom sat too, shuffling the food that had fallen on the tablecloth into her napkin.

I continued to stand, listening until every claw settled and the walls fell quiet again.

The rats stop now. I look up at the ceiling, waiting. Eventually, they begin to scrape again, running across the attic floor.

'Let me know if you find anything tomorrow,' I say to Jimmy.

'It's just strange,' he says. 'Your mom said he was disoriented, but she also mentioned he went out searching for someone.'

I pause. 'Did she say who?'

'Beats me,' Jimmy says. 'Just said he should've stayed in Vietnam.'

I thank Jimmy and hang up.

'Mom,' I say. 'What was Dad telling you again before he left?'

'Your father was unwell.' She sips her coffee. 'I've tried to tell you.'

'But what was he *saying* to you?'

Coughing, she brings her clenched hand to her mouth and rubs away stray spit. Her lipstick smears, whole chin smudged red. She then grabs another sugar packet and tears it with her teeth, pouring it into her mug.

'He was always looking for her out this window. That's why he built it, you know. Always talked about her when he first got back. It was better when you came around. But it started up again – I told you it had – he was talking about *her* again.'

'Was he searching for her?' I ask.

Mom stops stirring. She looks at me now. 'One time, when he first came back, I told him – only as a joke – but I told him if he ever left me for her, I'd kill him.'

My heart pounds. I can't help but stare at the empty seat behind Dad's cup.

'It was just a joke, but you should have seen his face.' A tiny laugh rolls out and plops into her coffee.

'Mom,' I say, slowly. 'Do you know what happened to Dad?'

Her hand opens on the table then and Dad's patchy brown handkerchief uncrumples. MTP has been cut out.

'He got lost in his memories,' she says. 'He got lost and I don't think he will find his way back this time.'

Small feet wash over the attic like waves swarming a rock.

(10, 190)

Cracks
Wester Wagenaar

All human life starts with a deafening wail, as if babies already know life will never get better than the warm, unconscious comfort of a belly. If I allow you to live, I'm confident you'll welcome life in the same way. Sure, there'd be plenty to cry about. I look at the pill in my palm and imagine the possibility of you. Maybe I wouldn't fuck it all up. Maybe you'd be my way out.

I imagine a world where I give birth to you. There, I find myself in a white hospital gown soaked through with sweat, still catching my breath from the worst physical pain of my life, staring at your crumpled, purple body crying out in desperation. The doctor carries you towards me, and you relax once I press you to my breast, close to the only home you have known. Your tears dry out, and I witness your scrunched, crescent eyes open as you see me for the first time. They are bright blue and flecked with gold, like your father's. I can't help but look away.

Nurses roll my bed to the postnatal ward, parking it alongside other mothers wrapped in identical hospital gowns. Most come with male extras, a rare few are alone like myself. A nurse drops by, hair a party of curls pulled into a professional ponytail, a list pinned to the clipboard in her hand. She tells me how to breastfeed for the first time, how to change your diaper, how to recognise and identify each noise you emit. You come with the same set of instructions as every other new-born.

I stop listening. Still dazed, I wonder why all hospitals share this aggressively clean, chemical smell. I appreciate it, this smell, so vastly different from my home's, recognising in it warmth and kindness and care.

A day or two later, we have to leave the hospital for my hell-hole of a flat in my hell-hole of a tenement. The gelled-up, bulging landlord sported a smile when I first showed interest, years before you entered my life.

'You won't find anything cheaper,' he said. 'Too small for pets though,' he added as if that was the worst he would admit about the place.

Supporting you with my right arm, I steer around silver canisters littered across the cobbled alleyway, then attempt to open the front door. Next, you're on your back on the sheets, an upside-down turtle, your bluish limbs wriggling like tentacles. I'm seated at the bed's edge, back arched, fingers covering my face, finding consolation in darkness. Burdened with the responsibility of my own life and yours.

I lift my head from my hands, facing the all too familiar grease stain on the peeling wallpaper. You're here, yet I feel alone. I miss the nurses whose faces still respond to birth like a miracle even after having witnessed it hundreds of times. I miss the midwives unrelentingly uttering, 'it'll be okay,' the phrase more familiar to them than their own name. And I miss the chemical clean smell.

I take a good look at you. Your arms are pudgy, maybe even fat, like water wings attached to your skin. Your hair is a thin brown, with a hairline that appears to have receded all the way to the crown of your skull. I can't criticise your face, that blank face, except for those bright blue goldstones in your sockets.

Everyone assumes mothers love their babies unconditionally from birth, but a part of me finds that difficult to comprehend. For the briefest of moments, I feel the urge to slip my fingers around your throat and push in my thumbs. The burning pain of guilt immediately follows, forcing me to pick you up and cradle you, tighter than before. It's a clumsy act to be expected from someone who used to run away from children.

I hope to see a smile, a comforting giggle. You swivel your head around, yet your lips remain closed, not even hinting at a grin. I pull you closer. You don't respond. I extend my arms, hands under your pits, and try to look at you directly. Unsupported, your head slumps to your chest like a sock puppet without a hand. You cry, more noise than tears, challenging your previous and only record thus far.

If only I had a £5 rock, I could forget about it all, at least for a short while. I whip out my phone and clench it until the plastic starts to creak. I swore I wouldn't; he swore he wouldn't take my calls. You're the reason why. I should be happy about being clean, but your incessant bawling makes it hard for me to think that.

You grow up angry. Tear-drenched, wailing sadness appears to be your favourite emotion, second only to boiling rage. When I try to tidy your toys, four-year-old you shouts, 'that's mine!' When I take a quick shower, I'm skipping soap because your toddler fists slam incessantly on the bathroom door. When I serve you veggies, you fling them at me by the handful or spoon catapult.

I'm on my laptop, trying to find a proper job to finally replace the waitressing ones I've been juggling. My thoughts are drowned by your pitter-patter footsteps; I'm doubting whether I should've taught you how to walk. You waddle across our tiny flat using your fists like wrecking balls, colliding with the dirty dishes I haven't yet put away. I've already learned it's no use responding with my own anger since shattering objects is the only thing that makes you laugh.

Again, I think of running to your dad for quick escapes, even though I know that's impossible. At one point I couldn't hide your existence from him any more and he lost it, furious because you were growing in my belly. He was the worst, a man-child, a scumbag, a piece of shit. But he was also my dealer whom I'd needed for so long. He made desperate attempts to persuade me, blackmailed me by saying he wasn't going to sell to me unless I took pills to obliterate you. I screamed in return, 'You think *I* wanted this?'

For a rare moment, you sit down, surrounded by the shards of dishware you smashed minutes before. I'm too tired to clean up your mess. You crawl over to your box of wooden blocks. You stack them and create the highest tower gravity allows before it topples. I turn back to my laptop and crack a rare smile. For once you don't act like a Gremlin.

I'm scrolling through the job ad for a hairdressing assistant when you erupt into a gleeful squeal. Before I know it, the picture of the wavy-haired model on the web page turns pitch black with an anticlimactic crunch. Cracks spread from the inside of the screen like a footstep on a sheet of ice, and I see one of your blocks sticking out of my laptop screen.

You're not a kid destroying dreams, as childless adults like to assert, teenage me proved perfectly capable of blowing them up herself – most of my life, my future was limited to when I could get my next hit of crack. I'm destroying *yours*, I realise, before you even have any dreams. I tried to get off drugs once I knew about your existence,

I really did. But when a woman gets knocked up by her dealer, even the sight of a positive pregnancy test can't get her clean overnight.

That's why, even if I do decide to keep you, even if you do allow me to clean up, you'll still be nothing but a crack baby.

No, I decide, now more confident than ever. Your story won't be lived. And so I find myself seated in a hospital room, skinny knees clattering like teeth in winter. I stare at the tiny pill in my palm, a round, yellowy-white tablet, 167 B divided between its two halves.

I can't stop swallowing back saliva. Before I take the pill, I phone him. Four rings, he picks up. 'And?' he asks. 'Yes,' I answer, my mind with you, still a lump of cells inside my womb. Pleased, his cold, steely voice turns sickly-sweet, asking if there's anything I want, anything he can sell me. My stomach churns, voice choking. My head fills with the desire to smoke crack, to again get off this world and drop back into the false relief of dreams. I force myself into wanting to tell him I don't intend to buy; not now, not ever. 'Fuck off,' is all I manage to mutter. I tremble when I press the red button on my phone and exhale in gasps.

I straighten my back, pill in hand, pick out the stains of the white wall, and think of the battle ahead.

Thank you. For giving me the strength to make a decision. For at least making me try to stand on my own two feet.

(2, 64)

The (Beep)
Milagros Lasarte

What is that sound that keeps her awake all night?

A short *(beep)*, high-pitched sound that comes and goes with a regular pattern. Three seconds of silence and *(beep)*. She has timed the intervals because she cannot fall asleep. Whenever she finds herself at the edge, one *(beep)* step away from slumber, the beeping pulls her back.

So, she lies there in bed, very still, eyes closed. She tries to determine whether the sound is coming from *(beep)* her left ear or her right. Two hours later, she still doesn't know. It switches, or she thinks it *(beep)* does. Sometimes it seems to come from within, deep inside her head, and she wonders if that is even possible. If your brain can make you hear *(beep)* things.

Things that are not there.

The first morning, when her *(beep)* alarm goes off, she dresses as fast as she can and rushes outside. The walk to her office soothes her; she can't hear a thing. Or rather, the rumble in the streets replaces the beeping. Perhaps it is still there, hidden under layers and layers of city noise. As it is, she forgets about it.

She forgets until she returns home to the vacant *(beep)* air of her flat.

She tries to ignore it and does *(beep)* everything she usually does, but a bit louder, so as to cover the sound – fool her brain into believing the beeping isn't there. And when she goes to bed, she is so *(beep)* exhausted she believes her fatigue will outwit the *(beep)*.

It doesn't work.

She turns and turns in her bed. Left *(beep)* ear. Right ear. Are you growing louder? Waves of vertigo *(beep)* strap her down to the mattress, leaving behind little beads of perspiration, but somehow, she finds the *(beep)* strength to get up. She switches the television on and sets the *(beep)* volume high enough for her to hear it from her bedroom. She focuses on that sound and eventually, hours after having first slipped under the covers, she manages to fall asleep.

When the alarm goes off on the second morning, she jumps up. Not entirely fresh but ready to tackle the new day. In the shower, she even sings a song. But then she makes the mistake of turning off the television and, after three seconds of silence, her tyrant returns.

(beep) The knife falls onto the table.

She pauses, turns around. Is she expecting to find someone there, hidden perhaps, playing a *(beep)* trick on her?

She calls in sick to work. She can't *(beep)* leave until she has solved this. Until she has found the source of the beeping. She *(beep)* scans her flat, standing motionless inside each room. *(beep)* She hears it every single time, but she can't see it. Where is the *(beep)* hiding?

It could be that the *(beep)* is loud enough to be heard through the walls. So, she asks *(beep)* the neighbours, the ones next door then those upstairs, if they have *(beep)* heard anything unusual. Anything like a *(beep)*? She isn't sure how to describe it. One has to hear it to understand. They tell her they haven't noticed a thing but will get in touch if they find something. She thanks them but doesn't expect to hear *(beep)* from them again. If they had encountered the *(beep)*, the signs would immediately show. It is impossible to hide that little tremor of the right hand, *(beep)* that shortness of breath. The *(beep)* invades the body slowly. First through the ears, then creeping its way to the eyes, the tongue – clouding every *(beep)* sense.

As a last resort, she proceeds to check all her appliances, turning them off then back on one at a *(beep)* time, but to no avail. So, she cuts off the electricity of the entire flat to make sure – the *(beep)* is still there.

Where are you coming from? With that robotic tone that makes you so unbearable, a touch so *(beep)* alien to anything I've heard before, and that metallic flavour that dribbles down my tongue.

Friends come to see her, worried about her absence and *(beep)* silence. They ask her if she is sick. She can neither confirm nor deny. She tries to explain the *(beep)* to them.

'Do you hear it too?' *(beep)*

'What are we supposed to be looking for?'

She doesn't answer. They would know if they heard it.

They urge her to see a *(beep)* doctor. She tries to explain the situation again, but she lacks the right *(beep)* words to describe what is happening, what she hears. The doctor thinks she knows what the cause may be. She prescribes some medication, just something to keep her calm, and *(beep)* sends her to see a specialist.

A whole week of tests and scans cannot kill the *(beep)*. With every test that denies a cause, she feels its presence growing, taking up more and more *(beep)* space, breathing her own air. Yet its consistency gives her hope. How can she hear something that doesn't exist? It is *(beep)* somewhere within her. It's only a matter of finding it, *(beep)* of fixing her. She tells them to check again and again. They *(beep)* say it's all in her head. So, she asks them to check her brain, open it up if necessary.

(beep)

They send her away.

Not even the television can drown the sound now. The *(beep)* manages to reach her, distorting noises so as to magnify itself. She barely sleeps, for even in her dreams the *(beep)* follows her. It likes to surprise her when someone is about to speak and what comes out of their lips is not a word but the *(beep)*. It hovers there, like a shadow looming over a body that has now grown weak. At times, she realises she is holding her *(beep)* breath, unsure why.

She cannot say what happens in all those hours she lies in her bed. It is possible she does get up, *(beep)* maybe to drink or eat something. It doesn't really matter anymore. She feels nothing but tired and the *(beep)*. It has taken a new form. It is now a sound wave that *(beep)* shakes her from within, and she flinches with every new *(beep)*.

The lack of sleep messes with her thoughts. She forgets things that happen and her *(beep)* brain can no longer find a chronological balance to her days. She knows time hasn't gone *(beep)* still because there are instances when the three seconds stretch and she hopes, could it be, is it over? It should have come, but I don't hear it – *(beep)*.

The blinds in her *(beep)* bedroom are closed so as not to see how the days go by and she does nothing. It's not that *(beep)* she doesn't try, but she cannot focus. If she attempts to read the *(beep)* overwhelms her and words lose their meaning.

No one comes to see her anymore. They are *(beep)* bored with what they assume is an act. They say she is exaggerating. That it cannot be that bad. Whatever it is *(beep)*, she can learn to live with it.

But she can't accept it. She cannot accept something that shouldn't *(beep)* be. So, she tries piecing back together that last *(beep)* day of silence, desperate to figure out if she missed something. If there was anything she could have done to prevent the *(beep)*. But the *(beep)* tells her it's useless. She should embrace it now.

It chose her, didn't it? Not the *(beep)* friends she had spent that day with or her colleagues. Not any stranger she had passed in the *(beep)* streets. She cannot defy it, and it takes advantage of her powerlessness, clinging to her body, to her *(beep)* existence, feeding itself on her.

Over time she becomes dependent on the sound. Expecting it to be *(beep)* there, hating when it is. It now marks a tempo that she cannot *(beep)* live without. And her brain is alert, looking for the *(beep)*, constantly, so that sometimes she hears it and realises she was actually *(beep)* waiting all along. Other times she sits up abruptly in her bed, opens her eyes and whispers into the darkness:

Are you still there?

(beep)

She lies back down, satisfied.

What was it like before, when there was silence? Did she make the most *(beep)* of that tranquillity? Ignorance had been a treacherous friend. And she blames herself, all the while acknowledging she couldn't have *(beep)* known. She could never have guessed that her entire existence would contract into this one individual moment in time, *(beep)* this dot in space. That they would become a unit – her and the *(beep)*.

In moments of rage, a cry escapes her *(beep)* lips. What do you want? What must I do to appease you? The *(beep)*'s answers are always cryptic.

(beep) And as she lies still in her bed, she thinks between two *(beep)*:

What if the *(beep)* only ends with my life?

What if it doesn't?

(beep)

(3, 196)

Diggin
Iona Zawinski

Lucy used tae paint. Now she digs tae forget. She likes the noise ay the sharp spade cuttin through the earth, like a sword enterin its sheath. There's skill tae it too – a basic understaundin ay physics bein a distinct advantage. It's aboot leverage, pressure, and a bit ay biology too. Ye cannie just go aroond flinging yer arms every which way, twistin or hunchin, fuckin up yer spine. Naw. Ye have to ken whit's goin on in there – in the body. Ye have to ken how tae strain it least, whilst shovelling maist. A delicate balance. Safe n efficient. Mindful ay the muscles. Lucy studied em, in er anatomy books. She kens aw their names.

Er steel-toed boot hovers above the right-hand side ay the blade before stampin firmly doon, a wee smile ay satisfaction creepin across the lines ay her face as it sinks tae the hilt. Then, gently, she rocks it back n forth, back n forth, hummin a wee lullaby as she goes. On the final rock back, she dips the handle doon tae almost kiss the groond n there's a wee crack – the pivotal point ay break-through, a tiny moment ay triumph – as the blade rises, well-heaped, intae the air. She steals a look, scans fer stanes, chopped worms, the composition ay the soil. Few stanes. Worm-free. Clayey. After a wee swing back, fer velocity, she launches it up tae er left, aff the spade n ontae the mound. It's barely a mound at this point. There's a long way tae go. At least 4ft. It's ahwiz much longer when it's a re-opener. The paths atween the rows ay graves bein sae narrow, ya cannie exactly just drive a JCB intae the middle ay em. So, ye've got tae dae the whole hing by haund, and run the risk ay The Crunch.

    Lucy huz heard it a couple ay times before, ahwiz folleyed by a short fall – the final few inches ay the full 6.8 ft. The first time, she got the boak – straight up spewed, aw oer er boots and the mixture ay splintered wood and bones they wur stood in. The crumbled dust ay some auld lad, patiently waiting on his widowed wife, now marinated in regurgitated Pot Noodle: Bombay Bad Boy. Lucy hud stood there – externally immobile, internally churnin – as if held back by an invisible haund. Upon release, she hud leapt fer the ladder – the cornerstone ay the whole operation, without tha, ye'r fucked – barely touchin the rungs in er scramble. She hud then stood above, pantin and starin, scratchin aboot in er pockets fer fags and a lighter – suhin tae calm the nerves. Yer first Crunch is ahwiz the worst. The memory ay the sound is smeared away wi the back ay er haund across er crumpled, moist brow that's ahwiz lookin sae tense.

    Lucy's face relaxes as she catches a metallic glimpse in er periphery. The ladder is in place, ay course. She grips the handle ay er spade, raises, and then drops it –

a stab in the earth – ready for another stamp, rock, swing. The lullaby bubbles oot ay er again, but just as the bow is aboot tae break – the one supportin the cradle, baby n aw – Lucy faws silent. She hinks she's heard suhin. Abruptly conscious ay er breath n tightenin chest, er heart rate surges. Er jaw clenches. The spade remains motionless, suspended mid-dig by rigid arms. She waits. Only silence. Well, naw, ay course no *silence*. There iz the faint bleatin ay Spring lambs on the wind, the rustlin ay leaves – churchyard trees, grown on the nutrients ay the deid – then, the quiet mutterings ay auld Morris, on iz daily visit. Awfie polite. Awfie pious. E's wearin the same paddy cap, scerf, jaickit, shoes and everyhin as normal. Aw shades ay broon: chocolate, chestnut, fawn... E huz a very particular style – a kinday neat shabbiness. Or mubbi, a shabby neatness? E isnae a scruff, but e iz a wee bit scruffy, ken? And e'll huv iz rosary beads tae, never seen wi'out em. Them wee bits ay wid must be rubbed tae the nub, the amount ay wear they get. Iz hairy-knuckled fingers, worryin and worryin at em. Praying fer wha? Aw the folk here are awridy deid. Surely judgement huz awridy been passed, if there iz any judgement at aw.

Morris doesnae seem tae huv noticed anyhin suspicious. There's nae break in the burble ay his chatter, or the fidgettin ay his fingers. He's workin his way up the row towards er. Wan grave at a time. Then they'll huv the exact same encounter as they ahwiz dae, as maist folk dae, wi

Morris. She can awridy feel his leathery palms against hers – the clasp, the long shake – as she huz a deek at him, eight graves doon. She can hear iz voice in er heid, like an auld bike in need of an oiling – squeaky and cracked tae fuck. Certainly distinguishin. And them electric blue eyes, shinin oot fae under his tangled grey caterpillars, starin straight intae hers.

'Peace be whicha, child. Peace be whicha . . .'

'Thank you, Morris. Thank you. Thanks. Ta very mu . . .'

As long as e held on, shakin and shakin, wishin ya peace in iz shrill Irish lilt, ye wid continue tae thank im. She wonders how long iz longest shake huz been. How many times wiz e thanked? How many times, in iz whole life, huz e wished a body peace? Thoosands, surely. E must be pushin seventy now. And how much guid huz it done? Impossible tae tell. At least e's tryin – auld Morris. Purest intentions. She's tryin anaw. But no really, no wi er heart. That stopped, then the art. Morris is a kinday artist, she hinks. Painting wi prayers. She resumes diggin.

The mixture ay shades in the soil gets er hinkin aboot Morris's funny wee ootfit: the clayey stuff is mair grey-ish brown, like iz cap; and the sandy stuff is mair beige, like iz jaicket; and then the reddish stuff, kinday like iz chestnut breeks. There's a portrait ay Morris in the layers ay dirt. She sees it. She wants tae paint it. She wants tae paint him. Why him? Appearin in the dirt like a prophet. But she only came here tae dig. And tae forget. Morris is daein the opposite – practically wagin a war on forgettin. The whole cemetery is. Aw those names. Carved intae stone. Long-lasting stone. But the aulder wans are fadin. The grooves shallowing out. Little particles ay stone-dust swept aff in the wind wi the bleats ay the lambs, year affer year. The auldest huv fallen oer and cracked, great splits through the thick slabs, leavin just pieces ay rock. Pieces ay rock, like ye'd ring a campfire with, or use tae bash in a tent peg in the absence ay a mallet.

Er arms uv got healthy burn in em. She takes a moment tae catch er breath, glance aboot. Morris's gettin closer. Back tae work. She's gettin deeper, bout 3 ft doon, using the ladder tae reach the mound up on the left mair easily. When Morris's finished wi Mr Bryce in the grave next tae er, e approaches slowly, a wee shuffle. A shy extension ay iz arm. Nae words. She lets oot a wee sigh, rests er spade against the wall ay er hole, and steps up the ladder. The usual exchange. But just as e lowers iz gaze and releases iz grip, she hawds on. Now she willnae let him go.

'Naw, peace be wi you, pal. Peace be wi you.'

She finds ersel sayin. He looks back at er wi iz bewildered blues. She's still no letting im go. This might nivir huv happened tae im afore.

'Tanks, child. Tanks.'

She grips harder.

'Naw, honest, ye deserve it, Morris. Ye deserve it. You're special, Morris.'

E's lookin a wee bit feart now.

'Naw really Morris, ye'r a top lad. And ye'r ma muse, y'ken tha? Ah'm gunna paint ya, ye hear that? I'm finally gonnae paint again. And it'll be you, 'cause you're sae pure. And ye can have it, once it's done, promise. Ye can hang it in yer . . . dae ye huv a hoose, Morris?'

E nods, tentatively.

'Perfect. Ye can hang it in yer hoose, Morris. Would ye like tha? A portrait ay yersel? Ah'd love tae dae it.'

She throws er maist expectant face at im. E doesnae ken whit tae dae, just stares at er, iz arm limp, hand still clasped in ers.

'A painting, Morris. Fer you. Of you. Ye wanih, aye? A present?'

E smiles.

'Ah child . . .'

She smiles back, relaxing her grip. His hand slides oot, free, n gies er a wee pat on er arm.

'. . . peace be whicha.'

E touches iz fingers tae iz lips and turns iz back. On tae the next grave.

Alveolus
Josh Wagner

In the Beginning . . .

She was sneezed into being. Floating between the beams, a thing in the dark.

And no matter what she would become later, those first inklings popped her cork to a wild blue yonder, establishing patterns she could never entirely escape. Generation after generation, defined by a futile ache for cohesion. A soul in search of a body.

First she split in two. Then four, eight, sixteen . . .

Soon she would flow like water, from one drop to another.

Then

Trillions of incarnations later, something amazing happens.

Now she's a little yellow light, one of hundreds, drifting between the summer leaves. Her skin crackles like magnesium shavings. In this form, the concept of 'I,' which has long been with her (like a tiny mental glow between the eyes) but whose reference she has never fully grasped, finally grasps its own reference. Maybe it's because now that she *is* a tiny glow, it's all started to – oops, snatched and eaten up.

On to the next.

When she wakes up she has become the same kind of thing that just ate her. Leathery and cold. Glossy eyes stare longingly into the sky. She fills her guts with swarms of former kin. Hungry to reconnect with herself, the 'I' grows more persuasive. Her jaws are strong. She licks at clouds. Later, she dies from a microbial invasion.

By the time she's up and walking around on four legs, the descendants of those invaders work for her – civilising her interior. Her nostrils are vestibules, her lungs furious with air.

Two legs now. Legions of new voices in her head struggle for control over the 'I' and its little light.

At night she wrings her hands. She aches for dissemination, to fill the empty spaces. To exist both down in the valley and up on the mountain, to sleep in the grass while also lost at sea. She hikes through forests at dusk, pursuing an endlessly receding horizon, mesmerized by the little floating lights who blink in and out of existence.

Something tickles her nose. She squeezes her eyes. A sharp intake of breath. From the darkness embers bloom – fracturing dawn's golden shell.

Now

Her dentist browses a tray of hard steel. He rattles off terms she's never heard and doesn't understand.

I don't care, just get it over with.

She takes prolonged breaths from the translucent crystal green mask, and accepts the 'pinch' of his needle as a necessary evil. It isn't as bad as she remembers. As a child, those damn shots would come in like a chainsaw.

The ceiling is a grid of beige tiles. The centre tile has been replaced by the oversaturated painting of an agrarian landscape whose peach sunset ignites stratocumulus clouds. In the field a lone oak stands firm. She recognizes this tree. Yes, this exact tree. She saw it last week in a vision – one of her funny little visions.

Ha ha.

She feels the incision but not the pain. It's a bit like someone drawing a line on her gums with a ballpoint pen.

Her dentist clacks the titanium jaws of forceps three

times in front of her face like some periodontal ritual.

To think this all started with a sneeze.

All her life, whenever she sneezes, her field of vision gets blasted shotgun-style by these temporary black holes. Through them she has witnessed wonders: bright colours and swirling patterns and grotesque creatures moving to and fro. Lasts a minute or two at most. Her close friends don't say *Bless you*, they say. *What did you see?* This time it was teeth. Fields and fields of teeth drifting in the breeze. Strings of teeth hanging from the branches of a lone oak. Yes, that exact oak.

The dentist swoops in and digs up part of a tooth. This surprises her, and she's surprised by her surprise. Of course it's a tooth. But when he rotates it under the light, she realizes it isn't a tooth at all. It's a proximal tarsal ossicle – the tiny bone of a baby bird.

A few minutes later, he emerges with a golden lump. Part of an old filling? Wait, not gold. It's copper. *The BB!* she thinks, transported back to the day her brother shot her. He hadn't meant to. It ricocheted and pierced her cheek. She'd promised to keep it secret. Apparently she'd kept the slug as well.

Next, her dentist draws loose a thin silver chain. She feels its anchoring pearl pop free. A gift from the inaugural boyfriend, who eventually cheated on her with the debate team captain and his sister. Bawled her eyes out in a Fred Meyer parking lot. Hurled the necklace at his vanishing taillights. Had she gone back for it and forgotten? Swallowed it down in some ritual of teenage sex magic revenge?

Here comes the coin she flipped to see who got to sit next to Arnold Fetcher. The coiled shell he brought back for her from Crete. The SD card she accidentally left in the class camera – the one with *those* pictures on it. The pink rabbit's foot she filched from her mother's purse on a road trip to South Dakota; her first crime, and a big stupid secret which, over time, extinguished any hope of genuine communication between them, as if something looming and dreadful blistered on the foot itself, wedging them apart.

She'd sneezed at the funeral. Seen herself in the casket.

Deeper and deeper goes the alveolar excavation. Here's a bit from when she clipped her dog's toenail too deep. A pinky ring from her first-grade best friend. Her fear of fuzzy caterpillars. The spontaneous orgasm at church. A rejection letter from Rochester. The same random numbers she always picks. A dream where she became the fulcrum at the rupturing base of the ocean. Her hope of overcoming all major weaknesses by forty-five. Every fingernail she's ever chewed off, along with her forsaken desire to stop. A lungful of pot smoke. The Amazon river. Keys from her daughter's future piano, one black, one white. Regrets and reconciliations she's yet to make. The job she'll wish she'd have kept. Her grandchildren's first everything.

The dentist pauses to check the x-ray. He spritzes something in the fresh cavity, and out come her final words. She feels them swirl around her cheeks. Bracing to launch off the tip of her tongue. She can't quite hear them, but there they go.

What do I say? What will I say?

'That's it!' says the dentist.

He shows her a healthy white dimpled crown, then flips it over to reveal a decayed black catacomb in the root.

'Nice one!'

Wait, shush.

She tries to shush him, desperately.

Her tongue probes inside the gaping hole. Feels a familiar tickle in the nose.

'Relax,' says the dentist.

He introduces the horrible suction tube to the inside of her gums. Its violent aspiration manages to catch the tail of those flighty final words and draw them back a bit. Her ears ache. She thinks she can almost hear. Her chest distends with a sudden gasp of air.

Not now, not now!

But she can't help it. The sneeze breaks forth, strong enough to splatter the moon, shattering her last words into their individual letters and blowing them all into hurricane swirls racing into the painting on the ceiling. She sees a 't,' an 'l,' a double 'e.' They slip between strands of barbed wire. Vowels tangle in the wild wheat, disintegrating on the withering leaves. A faint yellow light pulses among the fingers of the oak. Her lips part and re-join. Sunset's lustre starts to wane.

It's fine, she thinks. *One day, I'll remember it all, lying back in some old chair, nose twitching.*

And that day, gently, as if reciting ancient verse, each word will leap from her lips, and she will follow, free of flesh, far off and away across the mountains.

After & Before

In the end, fringed by darkness and cold, she has at last become everything. Yet she is now so diffuse that everything is little more than a series of unrelated impressions.

How long has this been going on? Trillions of years without the energy required for even the slightest iteration.

The more she wonders, the less her thoughts make sense. She's forgotten how it feels to change. Occasionally, certain ideas congeal and a feeble glow stirs in the void before slipping under the waves of memory. Soon the darkness will petrify to the point where even the faintest flicker would resemble the conclusion to some violent star.

If only there were still eyes to see.

For a moment, serenity settles over the surface of a black well. These eons have been one deep breath. A slow settlement of empty corridors. She feels a tickle behind her eyes. Her gasp as sharp as the nose of a fountain pen.

Embers erupt – billowing dawn's empty shell. Between ragged drapes of shadow looms a fractured golden light.

(1, 202)

Vex Hex
Ning Cai

'Venti iced skinny hazelnut macchiato, sugar-free syrup, extra shot, light ice, no whip,' I announce, carefully lifting the beverage from its flimsy cardboard carrier and setting it directly before Miss Bel. The tapping of her chipped nails against the boardroom table stops and she grabs her order, stabbing the straw through the top, not batting an eye at me.

'Triple, venti, half sweet, non-fat, caramel macchiato,' I say, handing the steaming drink to Mr Levi, who gives me a shadow of acknowledgement with a slide of his green eyes.

'How much longer do we have to wait?' Mr Tan growls, stroking his salt and pepper goatee as I put his drink (tall non-fat latte, 2% foam) in front of him.

'Boss is coming down from a meeting with Upper Management,' Mr Ma says, wetting his lips before slurping down his grande chai tea latte (three pumps of skim milk, no foam, extra hot). 'We should start soon. I too, have things to take care of after our meeting.'

'Frappuccino with extra whipped cream and chocolate sauce,' I mutter, passing the cup to Mr Bub, who has brought in a dozen sugar glazed doughnuts. All for himself, of course.

'Thank you, darling,' Mr Mo drawls, giving me a salacious wink as his fingers graze mine accidentally on purpose and he takes his usual (iced, half-caff, ristretto, venti, four-pump, sugar-free, cinnamon, dolce soy skinny latte).

Just as I set down the last beverage, the double doors of the conference room burst open and the glamorous hourglass figure of Miss Lu strides in. They all straighten up in their seats and I scurry to the side, picking up the water jug in my now clammy hands and standing with my back against the wall. My dark mop of hair covers half my face, but I'm secretly watching Miss Lu walking in those sexy Christian Louboutin heels

Miss Lu sighs as she slides into her chair, extinguishing her cigarette in the clean ashtray I had prepared for her earlier, then takes a long drink. Giddy with delight, I peek through my bangs, thrilled over how pleased she is with the caramel macchiato (venti, skim, extra shot, extra hot, extra whip, sugar-free) that I, a lowly intern, had fetched for her.

'Belphegor, Leviathan, Satan, Mammon, Beelzebub, Asmodeus,' she greets each demon with a professional nod of the head. 'Shall we begin?'

'Yes, Lucifer,' they chorus over a shuffling of papers.

'The Old Man is massively unhappy with our latest numbers,' Miss Lu starts as she lights up a new cigarette with the tip of her middle finger. She exhales and perfect smoke rings rise above our heads. 'Overpopulation is a big problem. Something needs to be done ASAP. C'mon people, I need ideas. Now!'

Mr Tan frowns as he scrubs his lobster-red face with equally red claws. 'I can expedite World War III?'

'Not enough time,' Miss Lu snaps. 'We need something fast, Satan. A war takes too long to put into effect, plus your boys have been failing to get any results since North Korea.'

'Zombie apocalypse?' Mr Bub quips, in-between mouthfuls of his glazed doughnuts.

'Requires too many resources, Beelzebub. You should know by now we're a family-run business with no fancy budgets,' Miss Lu rolls her eyes, shaking her pretty blonde curls. 'Jesus. Next!'

'Major stock market crash? We can easily project a fair number of suicides.' Mr Ma purses his lips. 'More folks will also start praying again. That should make our Lord happy.'

'Boring. Next!'

'Famine and drought?' Miss Bel offers.

'Locusts?' Mr Levi adds.

'Been there, done that. Next!'

'How about a plague? Something even more lethal than AIDS?' Mr Mo suggests.

'It would be faster to start World War III than to wait for those fuckers in R&D to come up with another incurable disease. Seriously, doesn't *anyone* have any new ideas?'

Miss Lu is officially pissed off now, and her beautiful face glows white with fury. She stubs out the cigarette between her painted lips, and with another sharp click of her fingers, artfully conjures up the much-dreaded Bagpipes of Doom.

'Don't make me now,' she warns, as the demons flinch. 'Ideas, people, ideas!'

But they have nothing and cower like trapped animals. With a sadistic smile, Miss Lu rises the mouthpiece of that terrible instrument to her crimson red lips and sucks in a deep breath.

'Wait!' I cry. 'I-I think I've got something…'

Silence fills the room as everyone turns to stare at

me, noticing my insignificant presence for the very first time.

'Who in bloody hell are you?' Mr Tan demands, his face now even redder than usual. 'And what exactly do you do here?'

'I'm an intern," I wince. "I get coffee and stuff?'

'You mentioned you had an idea?' Miss Lu squints, and I feel my heart turn to mush under her gaze.

I nod my head furiously. 'Vaccines!'

Everyone exchanges looks. Miss Lu arches an eyebrow at me.

'Keep talking, minion.'

'Well, anti-vaccines really,' I say as I put down the water jug, talking with my hands. 'We basically spread a rumour amongst mankind that vaccines are bad. Create an anti-vax movement planted by hoaxed scientific studies, championed by paranoid moms who believe big pharma conspiracy theories, along with those vocal has-beens who miss their fifteen minutes of fame. Unvaccinated humans get sick, they die, the ones around them spread the sickness, even more die. This solves the world's population explosion problem, right?'

The bagpipes vanish. Miss Lu gives me a dazzling

smile of approval, and excitement buzzes through the room.

'Welcome to the club, kiddo,' Miss Lu purrs as she magicks up a shiny new name tag which floats over and pins itself on me. Looking down at the gold piece, I beam with pride.

VEX.

(8, 148)

The Fox is in the Wing of Sector 4
Ning Cai

'Oi! Watch it!' I scold the hunchback in rags pushing past me, but the old coot continues down the cobblestones, worldly possessions rattling inside a sad tartan suitcase.

Squeezing the small metal piece in my fist, I hasten towards Edinburgh's infamous "pubic triangle" of strip clubs, entering a relic of a hotel by Bread Street. 'Arlen Scott, MI5,' I tell the lad at the check-in counter. I show him what's in my hand. 'This yours?'

'Aye, agent. Where yer found it?'

'St. Cuthbert's,' I grunt. My partner had tracked down The Fox but I had gotten his message too late. When I reached the deserted cemetery, Kai was dead and I had to pry the key from his cold, stiff fingers. 'Occupant still inside?'

He nods and I make for the room. It all ends tonight.

Gun drawn, I enter, confident of having the element of surprise on my side. But there is no one there.

The room is untouched, save for a fancy box with ribbons on the bed. My name is written next to a kiss marked in crimson lipstick. I flip the lid, only to find a lusty pair of Jimmy Choos and luxurious lingerie in my exact size, along with my favourite perfume. But how?

'Looks like she's gone, Ma'am!'

Startled, I turn around and glare at the lad from the check-in counter. '*She*?'

'Foxy Asian lady, with a hipster bag.'

I arch an eyebrow. 'Tartan?'

He nods.

Patting the pockets of my jacket, I pull a wry grin. She has my wallet and ID. The chase continues.

To the Moon
Nicole Christine Caratas

Waxing Gibbous

I first fell in love with you when I was fourteen. My boyfriend thinks I'm crazy, I know. But we're sixty percent water anyway, so what does he expect will happen?

It was a gray night.

No it wasn't. It was just a night. I was gray.

That night, I learned that 'no' means 'yes.' I saw the rage in a man's bright green eyes.

I dragged myself home afterwards. My body ached in places I didn't know could ache. I couldn't look down at my feet out of fear I'd catch a glimpse of my body and remember. So my eyes fixed on the sky.

You weren't quite full yet. Just a lopsided blob. I felt my soul pull towards you like a spring tide. I hadn't cried until that moment. You were the most beautiful thing I had ever seen. You smiled down at me and told me it would all be okay.

I'm going to make it to you one day.

Full Moon
==========

I'm twenty-three when I meet my boyfriend for the first time. I'm sitting on a park bench, staring up at you, blinded by how bright you are tonight. I have headphones in with nothing playing. I'm crying.

> He asks what is wrong. I keep my eyes glued to you as I answer.
>
> 'It's just beautiful. Don't you think?'
>
> 'The moon?' He sits next to me. 'Yeah, I guess so.'
>
> Silence.
>
> 'But that's nothing to cry over.'
>
> 'But it is,' I tell him.

I'm not totally sure what it is about him. Probably his dark brown eyes. He doesn't understand, not that I can expect anyone to. But I let him walk me home.

Waning Gibbous
==============

I've always wanted to be an astronaut. I've never outgrown that dream. My vision is shit, though. And I have a bad back. And blood pressure lower than the Dead Sea. But I still need to get to you. I need to be with you.

'It's just a stupid rock,' he rolls those brown eyes at me. Though I can't see them, I know how they darken.

I'm standing on the balcony, looking at your reflection on the water in front of me. I'm failing to hold back tears. Again.

It's unfair. That you get to be so powerful. It hurts me to think of how strong you are. How steady. How constant. Look at the way the ocean obeys your command. So much depends on you.

How can I be like that? How can I channel that strength? How can I rise mighty like you? Be the maestro of symphonic waves in the nighttime?

'Stop crying,' he scoffs. 'You always fucking cry. I don't get it. It's so stupid.'

'She can move the oceans,' I whisper.

And yet, you're up there, without anyone. The occasional visitors. A singular flag. But all alone. The closest companions are 238,900 miles away.

'But she is still all alone.' I brush away a tear and move to face him.

I see your light in the glass door behind him. It's almost like you're here with me. An illusion of proximity that I cling to, for just a moment.

He turns from me and moves towards the stairs, leaving for a cigarette. He mutters something that sounds like 'it's not a she,' but he's gone before I can say anything.

Third Quarter

When I was twenty, I found someone. I thought he could understand me like you do. So I told him about my love for you. He was the first person I shared you with.

He and I thought we could mold each other into the people we wanted to be in love with.

He wanted an obedient wife. He wanted dinner on the table when he came home. He wanted me to love his mother and to remind him of important dates in his friends' lives. He wanted someone he could smack around when work life got tough, and a shoulder for those blue eyes to cry on once he was done and ashamed.

I just wanted someone I could count on, a perigee.

He used my love for you against me. With every slap came a declaration that he loved me deeply. With every 'to the moon and back, one thousand times,' I became less like you.

I strayed so far away from you then. It was the easier path to take, to leave you instead of him.

Waning Crescent

I stopped telling people about you after that. It seemed like everyone had an interest in you. Everyone thought you were so beautiful. Everyone loved you.

But they don't know you like I do. They never will. So I'll keep you to myself.

New Moon

You are looking down at me. I can feel it. You want to help me. You love me the way I love you.

I tell you about him, tell you that you shouldn't be offended that he doesn't like you. That he thinks no man has ever actually visited you.

I can hear you laughing.

You think he's bad news. You think I can do better.

I tell you I'm lonely. I tell you if I could move oceans, I'd do better.

But I can't. And he's not that bad. So I'll settle. For him.

'Stop crying and get your ass in here,' he yells from the couch. 'The sushi's here.'

He doesn't care that I am in the middle of a conversation with you.

I wipe my face off and meet him inside the living room.

He asks how I'm feeling. As if he suddenly cares.

Powerless, I want to say. *Alone. Like you should do something more. Learn to hold me like moonlight. Learn to be present regardless of how empty or full you are that day.*

Instead, I say 'I'm okay. I'm just hungry. And tired.'

There's the faintest flash of light outside. You're winking at me.

He hands me the bottle of soy sauce. He never remembers that I hate soy sauce. I pour myself a splash.

If only I could move an ocean. Even just one. Then he wouldn't be able to tell the difference between me and you.

Waxing Crescent

I leave the curtains open that night. The perfect view of you. He climbs on top of me. I breathe heavily as I turn my head away from his dark eyes and towards you instead. I moan his name into your face.

You know exactly what I feel in this moment. A wink.

He's asleep now. My fingers trace the lines on his back, but I feel your rilles.

Another flash of light. Your moonbeam settles on my skin. Are you calling me to you?

I leave the bed and walk onto the balcony again. You're giving off more light than you should be at this point.

I see the slightest movement on your face, like a breeze over a lake. Can those be waves? Or do you cry for me too?

First Quarter

I can feel you by my side the next morning after he's gone to work. You're halfway whole. Reaching total control. I wonder how much the shape of you affects how hard you pull the tides. I like to think that's how it works.

I want to be as strong as your fullness. I want to be that finishing half. It's my turn to conquer an ocean.

'No,' you tell me. 'I don't conquer them. I help them. I give them a boost. In return, they keep me company.'

Power doesn't equate loneliness after all. Not for

you, at least. So why should it for me?

<u>Waxing Gibbous</u>

He'll come home this evening to an empty apartment. I'll leave him a note.

> *Find me up among the planets,* it'll say.

He'll call me and find my number is disconnected. He'll ask my friends. They won't know what it means either. He'll think he sees me in every coffee shop, on every train, on every sidewalk for the rest of his life. But he'll never find me. Never again

<u>Full Moon</u>

I'm with you now. Just me and my moon. Goodbye.

(5, 197)

Atqasuk
Marc Berry

Men chased reality in cabins. London, Emerson, Muir, Thoreau – they all looked for nature's mandate to feel exuberantly and unequivocally alive. That's why I left home, why I travelled thousands of miles to Atqasuk, Alaska, where I first landed and stayed. It was a small town, a couple hundred or so people. I wanted to wake up. But Atqasuk did not wake me up. The people were all friendly, generous; there was a community that could one day feel like home. Yet, I was not ready for a home. Someone realised that eventually and pointed me in the direction of Wyatt. They told me he had a cabin out in the wilderness. That same evening, I went and saw him.

He was an old man. Grey hair, a long well-kept beard. Skin sagged at his eyes and his face showed signs of a weathered life. He insisted on sharing a cup of coffee or tea until I relented. He asked me why I wanted the cabin, asked how I would get there. He offered me an old snowmobile for cash. I said I would return that evening and left him mulling over his coffee.

That night, Wyatt's door swung open before I could knock on it. He invited me in; the fire was lit in the corner. I entered and followed him to the table in the centre of the room. I stayed standing as he sat back at the table, the day's paper still open in front of him.

'It's not practical, you know,' he said.

I asked him what he meant.

'This dream you have,' he paused until he found the right words. 'It's not practical. It's not a life. Out there on your own. It's a fantasy.'

'What else is there?' I bit back at him.

'I know what you're going through,' he said as he played with his beard. 'When the fire sparks and you flinch. When the dogs bark as you walk by and you jump a little. The way you close your eyes and shake when a plane flies overhead. I've seen it before.'

I glared at him as anger swept over me, remaining silent.

'I mean no harm, son,' Wyatt stood from his chair. 'I just want you to know nothing good will come from being alone. You won't find the answers you're looking for.'

I crossed my arms and stood up tall. Who was he to claim to understand what I was dealing with? He'd probably never left Atqasuk, let alone Alaska.

Wyatt pushed his chair under the table and walked across the room until he stopped at a small cabinet against the back wall. There was a vast array of keys hanging down, all numbered and labelled. Hanging among them was a dog tag.

'Here's your keys son,' Wyatt said.

I threw the envelope with just about the last of my cash on the table and took the keys.

'I'll take payment for the snowmobile,' he said, counting the money. 'But I don't want any for the cabin. So, if you have extra money in that envelope, take it out now.'

I didn't, so I stood in the doorway fiddling with the keys in my hand.

'Okay,' he said, holding his hand out for me to shake.

I shook it.

'Go find one of the brothers, you know who I mean right?'

I nodded. I'd been out on one of their wilderness tours before, but we had not gone far.

'They'll take you to the cabin. You might have to chuck them some money. They'll tell you what you need to bring before you go on your expedition.'

I nodded again, thanked him and started to walk out

the room, only stopping in the doorway.

'Those tags, are they yours?' I asked him.

'From my son. He never really came back from the war. He wanted to be alone too. We found him on the plain three months after he returned. He'd found his peace.'

I stood in silence, unsure what to say to the man. In the quiet that followed, he reopened his paper. I took my cue and started to the door.

'I hope you can find your peace out there too,' he said as I opened the door.

I found the brothers early the next morning. They ran a hiking and exploring shop. Knew the area better than anyone else, or so they advertised. They gave me a list of things I needed to collect or buy. Half the list was from their store.

I left with the eldest brother just before noon, following behind him on Wyatt's snowmobile. We arrived at the cabin an hour and a half later, stopping a couple of times for him to tell me the best routes to take. He helped me unpack my stuff, asked me one final time if I really wanted to go through with it. I nodded. He sat me down and explained the best way to keep warm, keep the cabin cosy, keep the snowmobile running and ready at all times. It was boring, but I'd grown accustomed to long, boring talks in the army. Before he left, he gave me an old hunting rifle. He told me the one in the cabin would quit working after a good hunt; it had been left unused for too long. I thanked him, and he wished me luck. When he left, the cabin settled into silence, and I was finally alone.

I remember reading long ago that the brutality and emptiness of the wilderness reduces life to its very essence. Survival. I realised this very early on in that cabin, that the wilderness was a kind of bridge between the modern world and an alternative, primitive one, a world which drew me in. Here, the veneer of civilisation was thin. In the cabin, I was free. I courted this suffering of the more primitive in the hope that my struggle would bring me closer to a fundamental aspect of reality. Through time, I understood the harshness of the wilderness. The freezing evenings when I couldn't get the fire started, the hunger in my stomach when I couldn't catch any game for days on end, the cabin brought me closer to reality than the cities or people could ever have done.

Today is the shortest day of the year, the longest night. The snowy peaks in the distance, far past the rivers and dead trees, will be light for a few hours. The sun's rays will tinge the snow-covered slopes with a deceptively warm-looking shade of orange. It has been eight months since I first came to the cabin. Fifteen months since I got honourably discharged. Thirty-two months since my father died. Thirty-six months since my mother died. Seventy-two months today since I first offered my body to my country.

I wake before the sun has risen. I light a candle either side of my bed. The flames flicker (against) the morning darkness. I can see my breath leaving my mouth, and I shiver as I begin to read my book. Often, that's all there is to a day. A little bit of movement, a little bit of light, and we call it a day. But I soon realised that a lot of life is like that. Some movement, some light, and another day has gone by. I spend my days in quiet, in the unknown world.

I get out of bed after an hour of reading. I tend to the fire and get it going. I light a propane lamp that hangs inside and start to make myself breakfast. It's uniform and uninspiring collecting blueberries, cranberries and kale during the short summer, but it's necessary to have food for the winter. Learn or starve, but I learnt. I eat my bowl of oats in silence. I prefer the silence. No loud noises, no sudden bangs or flashes. Nothing to take me back.

(10, 208)

Chinatown
Ting Yu Li

A row of yellow-brick houses near Peking University formed a line between the entrance of the University and Wanquanhe Street. Inside one of the houses lives Chou Ming's family. His father is an eminent history professor whose radical views oppose eradicating bourgeois representative figures within the Communist Party. In the living room, Father is drafting a Dazibao to protest the committee's discharge of the dean.

A radio is broadcasting in the background: *Great Chairman Mao is meeting with our most loyal comrade, Edgar Snow, at the Great Hall of the People.*

'Dinnertime!'

Mother brings out salted fish, sweet-sour pork rib, fermented tofu, stewed beef, and fried chicken with ginger and onion.

'Wow, we have pork rib?' Ming says. 'It's been a month since I've eaten pork.'

'Uncle Lin gave us some,' Mother says.

She pats Father's shoulder to remind him it's dinnertime. Father turns off the radio and goes to the kitchen to fill three bowls with rice. The kitchen is neat, with all the utensils arranged by size and function. The stew is served with a soup ladle and the rice in small bowls.

As usual, dinner starts silently because Father believes it's proper etiquette to eat quietly. Ming always doubts it, but his focus is reserved for the stewed pork now. He dips one pork cube into the sweet brown sauce, eats it whole, and quickly stuffs a spoonful of rice into his mouth.

'Did you pack all your stuff? School has granted me five days of leave next week,' Father says.

Ming glances at him. He thinks to himself that there is no way Miss Jin will let him leave because there is a middle semester exam next week.

'Do we have to leave for San Francisco? We don't have relatives there. Maybe after a while, they will let you go back to teaching?' Mother asks.

'No. A revolution is about to happen, and it will be no good for us. You heard them. We are the bourgeois now. We are the enemy of the proletariat.'

Ming can't tell if his father is joking. In truth, he doesn't even know what class he should be. He and his best friend Wang Yue were naturally assigned to the capitalist class since they possess some English books. Ming doesn't know if belonging to the capitalist class is good or bad, but before he can ask, Mother sends him away to finish packing. Instead, he goes to find Wang Yue. He walks to Wang Yue's house, and they meet outside of the door.

'We're late.' Wang Yue urges Ming to run faster to the nearby Hutong, where about twenty kids have already formed two groups: the paper top-hat group and the flat-cap group. Wang Yue and Ming take the paper top-hat from the big kid.

'Why do we fight them?' Ming asks.

'Those factory kids tore up our English books,' said Wang Yue. 'We fight for knowledge.'

The fight starts ruthlessly, and after a couple of tussles, Ming takes Wang Yue to escape from the chaos. Before parting, Ming promises to bring more English books and a real top hat for him, while Wang Yue swears to him that they will be best buddies forever.

The next morning Ming is packing with his parents. His mother tries to stuff most of the kitchen utensils into a huge plaid luggage bag. Ming drags a medium fabric bag to his room where soldier toys are piled up at the corner, all jumbled up with the dinosaurs and textbooks. He decides to give his toys to Wang Yue so that when he comes back they can play together again.

The living room is emptied of the usual decorations;

even the fake plastic rose on the television table is gone. But Chairman Mao's picture still hangs over the television.

The next day, at 5:30 a.m., Mother wakes Ming up and helps him into his clothes. A black sedan is parked outside their front door, and the driver is Uncle Lin. All the way on the road, Ming is asleep.

There aren't many passengers around when they arrive at the train station. Uncle Lin accompanies them all the way to their compartment. While Father and Mother busy themselves with the bedding, Ming wonders how Wang Yue will react when he gets the toys from Aunty Lin. A strange melancholy rushes to his eyes and tears begin to drop. He quickly rubs them away with the back of his hand.

The train runs south. As it gets closer to Guangzhou, more passengers get on the train speaking Cantonese. Ming notices men wearing suits with gold watches on their wrists and women in colourful dresses.

They get off at Guangzhou train station, where a slim man welcomes the family. With no time to rest, the slim man drives them to Panyu dock where they hop on a speedboat. Ming watches the water, the sparks, the waves, listening to the hypnotic sound of the engine. It is all new.

'Here is Tuen Mun wharf. Take a taxi or bus to Kowloon Walled City. Leslie is waiting for you there.'

'Thank you,' Father says.

Ming likes Kowloon Walled City a lot because it looks like a castle that remains standing strong after the enemy has tried to burn it to ash. It is shaped with layers on layers and each floor contains countless rooms squeezed in different shapes, eventually merging into an indestructible castle with thousands of inhabitants.

A stout man rushes from the dark alley near the entrance. He speaks in broken Mandarin asking us to follow him to room number 4.

Ming doesn't want to go to the room as he spots some kids in the playground and wants to play with them. But he is dragged away by Mother who also gives a warning glance. The room is shabby with mouldy walls, only one small television is playing Hong Kong news in English. A line of incandescent lamps illuminate the huge bed where the three of them will sleep tonight. None of them takes a shower. Maybe they want to keep the smell of home.

At night, Ming hears the muffled voices of his parents deep in conversation in the other room.

'What can you do in San Francisco?' Mother asks.

'I told you, I have an old professor there. He needs a research assistant.'

'Will that be sufficient for the whole family? I don't

know what I can do in such a foreign country.'

'Don't worry. I will look for jobs for you. It's a free country.'

'Nowhere is better than home.'

'We can come back after couple years. When the revolution is over.'

Ming is too sleepy to hear more but, in his dream, San Francisco is colourful, with speedboats like a story he has read in the science book.

Everything is sort of blurred at the moment he gets off the plane, only the sunshine sneaks through the gaps between his fingers. When they are out, a lot of people of different colours are packed in a small airport.

'Over there, over there.' Father drags Ming through the crowds, till they reach an older white man. They have a long conversation in English which Ming doesn't understand, but, based on their gestures and expressions, imagines goes something like this:

Old White Man: *Long time no see, my old friend.*

Father: *Did you keep my toy?*

Old White Man: *Of course. It's been such a long time I thought you would never come back.*

Father: *Such nonsense. I had to come back to continue my schooling.*

Old White Man: *Starting from sixth grade?*

Father: *Maybe, I don't know. Do you want to play the dinosaur-soldier game first?*

When they finally stop talking, the old white man leads them outside. He manages to find his car among lines and lines of cars. Ming and his mother squeeze in the back seat where all of their luggage has already taken up most of the space.

They drive down a long, straight, infinite highway. Ming is bored by the flatness of the landscape. At last, a huge bridge appears on the horizon, and Father turns his head back around to explain.

'This is the most important landmark of San Francisco, the Golden Gate Bridge.'

San Francisco begins to emerge. Ming sees cars of different colours; whereas in China cars only have two colours, either grey or black. Houses along the highway with rectangular windows, flashing signs sticking out from the ground. Beaches. The sea. Incredibly steep roads. Long-haired men walking together. When Ming starts to count how many long-haired men they pass, they arrive at destination - A Qing dynasty style green arch gate with a horizontal tablet: 天下为公 (the whole world as one community). The white man comes out from the car and says to them, 'Welcome to Chinatown.'

(6, 207)

The Immortal Science
James Alex

'Arthur,' said Daniel to his brother, dragging out the last vowel so it hung in the air as a whine. 'What is the Immortal Science?'

Great, thought Arthur. He had been back in Hopeton for twelve hours, and his wee brother was wanting to know what the rabid Stalinist outside of the auction was on about.

'I told you not to listen to that man,' said Arthur. 'He's full of shite.'

'Is it a thing you learn about in High School? It sounds like it might be cool.'

'It's not cool. It's a bad thing folk used to go on about.'

The only immortal thing about the Immortal Science of Marxism-Leninism here in this small Scottish town was that the proponent Peter Grieve refused to die: he was at least ninety.

Daniel had demanded they sit in the first row for when the auction was read out. The boy swung his legs restlessly while looking around the threadbare hall: sun faded posters for the latest parliamentary election still hung on the walls from three years ago, floorboards creaked with the weight of those in attendance, and intercom speakers buzzed with faint voices. People were filing in to sit behind them.

Much had changed in Hopeton since Arthur had left it at the age of eighteen, so characters like Grieve still wandering the streets kept his memories in check. Peter Grieve was the node of Windmere Street where he had grown up. Grieve was connected with a dozen other characters of the town: Davey Half-Head, who was walking in, had been hit by a car down by the river at the age of eight and had developed an uncanny ability to name winning horses; Melinda Lovenport, the thirty-year-old often witnessed in the north of the town, laying out a Dungeons and Dragons board in the seat behind them; and Kev O'Keith, who was fine to speak to, but was currently engaged in a conversation in the corner with a friendly ghost. Arthur would give any of them a nod if he was to pass them in the streets but wouldn't speak with them.

'Did you see that Stone Cold is the WWF champion now?' said Daniel.

'No,' said Arthur. 'I don't watch WWF.'

'Oh. What are you doing in school?'

'I'm doing a big thing about a man named Cézanne.'

'Oh. I don't know who that is.'

'He painted things a long time ago. Like Jack Smithson who did all those paintings of Hopeton.'

'Him that got done for looking at wee girls?'

'Aye, like him. But a lot better.'

There were sixteen years between Arthur and Daniel. They didn't have much in common, so all their conversations were grounded by the odd people of the town who were still stuck in their ways.

In the auction were LP discs from forgotten Thrash Metal bands, piles of books, and a few other items that had to go. Arthur didn't want to look at any of it. An LP was sold, and two books from the pile.

The final item was Frederick Husting's prized collection of photographs. Two years before Arthur was born, his father Frederick had been noted as having a 'poetic eye' in precisely one national newspaper. He developed his art throughout the years: he took photographs of the places his young family would holiday at, and then the grounds surrounding the offices he worked in afterwards. In his later years, before the inoperable brain tumour appeared, he documented the town he lived in: recording the starkness and rawness of life there, the austere conditions of the decaying community, the gnarled street kerbs and closed mills making up the dull husk of a once prosperous industry.

His educated son noted there were never any people in his pictures. His father always focused on the locales of the people, their houses, the derelict blocks of flats, which had since been demolished. All that was left was a slight memory in the minds of a few, and the photographs Frederick had taken which, if preserved, could last forever. But he always looked past the people to look at the houses they lived in.

Why were people absent from his photos? His father may have been shy about taking photos of people. Arthur was left with this question in the wake of his father's death. And of course, the sizeable gambling debt his father had racked up, that had to be paid off through selling everything and anything . . .

The elder Hustings had taken thousands of photographs but would throw away any he didn't deem perfect. In the auction were the remaining ones inside of a battered leather-bound photo album, totalling about a hundred photographs of the town as Frederick had found it throughout the years.

The bidding started at five pounds. Several people had glanced over the photo album, so there were more bids placed this time. First, the value of five was accepted, which was then bested by seven pounds, going up to ten, fifteen, twenty, before the bidding came to a halt. Twenty pounds for the collection of photographs.

It was Peter Grieve, the guy who had been shouting outside, that had bought them. Arthur baulked at the thought his Dad's best work would remain with such a man. At least they would be well looked after for the rest of eternity.

'Twenty pounds for those isn't bad!' said Daniel as they left.

'Compared to all of this other crap it's not,' said Arthur.

On the way home, they stopped at the local fish and chip shop next to the closed swimming pool. The food came to ten pounds in total, and Arthur spent ten pounds on petrol for the moving van. This was all they had to show for their Dad's life work: forty years of art auctioned off for fish and chips.

They sat in the van outside of their mother's house to eat. Daniel bit into the battered fish. 'Do you think Dad was good to us?' he asked between bites.

Arthur bit into a chip. He wasn't sure their dad had been good to them. But Daniel was ten. So, Arthur said, 'Of course he was good, we got this food because of him.'

(7, 200)

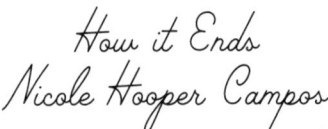

How it Ends
Nicole Hooper Campos

I leaned over the white sink with my toothbrush and spat. Red.

Is that . . . ? I blinked to clear my vision from the steam still lingering in my bathroom. Blood.

Great, I was officially dying. *Why did I move to Scotland again? Historical research?* Now I doubted I'd even make it to a library again. Much less see that book published.

Headaches, coughing, endless snot. The doctor still said it wasn't serious enough to merit an appointment. Just go for a consultation at the pharmacy they said. Ridiculous.

I was a former teacher for goodness sake. Hadn't I already spent years getting every possible disease children carried? Why were there still more?

Just then, a shrill scream came from the living room and I jumped in panic. I opened the door a crack and realised it was just my flatmates watching some horror movie across the hall.

Gripping the sides of the sink, I sighed and shook my head. *Pull yourself together.*

Three part-time jobs, a crazy landlady who blamed my dogs for everything wrong in the flat, and an essay to finish. I didn't have time to get sick.

'You are not sick.' I glared at the mirror. *Just pretend and it will go away.*

Making my way over to my bedroom, I heard my two flatmates cough. Yes, at the same time.

I opened the top drawer next to my bed. Pulling out the boxes of paracetamol, ibuprofen, and Sudafed, I looked inside. Empty. Fine. Pharmacy consultation it was. I closed the drawer and my copy of *World War Z* smacked me in the face. *Ugh.*

Fixing it on the shelf, I grabbed my keys and wallet and slipped into my boots. My dogs, giant husky mixes named Fred and George, looked at me expectantly. George held a ball in his mouth as if saying 'Play with us, mom.'

'Not now guys. When I come back. Okay?' They whined and I shuffled out the door. Thank goodness the bus stop was right in front of the flat.

The bus pulled up, and I swiped my card. A child in the front coughed without covering her mouth. A man in the back blew his nose full throttle. *Let's try upstairs.*

I walked past the rows, aiming for the back of the bus. A red-eyed lady. A coughing man. A sniffling teenager.

Make that two coughing men. Another man sneezed and wiped his nose with his sleeve. *Gross.*

I sat down and leaned my head against the window.

'As flu cases surge, death toll rises . . .'

A woman across from me stared at a video playing on the tiny screen of her phone. Unlike most people, she had forgone the use of headphones, treating everyone within hearing distance to the news playing from her phone's speakers.

'The Royal Infirmary has reported ten flu-related deaths in the past month from the Edinburgh area alone. Residents are strongly encouraged to wash their hands to break the chain of infection and obtain a flu jab as flu season gets underway . . .'

A few more people blew their noses and coughed. A woman squirted a giant glob of hand sanitiser onto her hands.

Well, at least the news is taking a break from politics. I hit the stop bell on the bus and went downstairs.

'Cheers,' I nodded to the bus driver and stepped off.

Five minutes' walk to the pharmacy from the bus stop. W*hy does it seem like such an eternity?* One step. Two steps. A girl walking in the opposite direction sneezed and groaned as she passed.

She sounds great. I gave her a wide berth.

Finally, I stood only a few paces from the pharmacy. The bell above the door clanged as I opened it. A woman with a blonde bob wearing black trousers and shirt smiled politely at me.

'Can I help you with something?'

'Well apart from feeling like I'm on my death bed,' I paused for a second, wondering if she'd laugh with me at my plight. Gallows humour and all. When she simply stared at me expectantly, I continued to list my symptoms.

'How about we get you on some paracetamol and Sudafed? It's been absolutely flying off the shelves.'

Great, just more of the same. I could have gone to the supermarket for that.

'Also, to clear those sinuses, maybe you should try some menthol crystals.'

Meth crystals? My brain stumbled over that information. *Surely, I'm not that far gone from the world of the living. Did I mishear?*

'What are those?' I asked.

'They're a type of aromatherapy. You dissolve a few into hot water and waft the steam towards your nose.'

'Ah, right. Well, I'll take the Sudafed, paracetamol, also ibuprofen, and some of those . . . crystals.'

'Okay.' She pulled the boxes off the shelf, then reached for a small container in front of the register and handed them all to me. I read the container label. 'Menthol.'

Ah, so they don't actually prescribe the hard stuff here in Scotland.

I paid and made the slow trudge back to the bus stop. One Sudafed, two paracetamol, one ibuprofen. I pulled out my water bottle. *Do I look like a drug addict?* A woman at the bus stop looked at the pills in my hand and then quickly looked away. *Apparently, I do.* I shrugged and swallowed.

A scream came from across the street and immediately people rushed towards a woman lying on the ground, surrounded by her shopping bags. I took a step forward then stopped. *What can I do?* The woman moaned and began to thrash madly on the ground.

I took a step back. *No, this isn't happening. Is it? But it only takes one. One person. One person to spread the infection.*

The bus pulled up and I ran on, breathing a sigh of relief as it pulled away. Away from the woman writhing on the floor. Away from the innocent people surrounding her trying to help. I drummed on the seat in front of me. Home couldn't appear fast enough. The news clip from earlier played in my head. So, for once the news wasn't simply being dramatic? *What am I going to do now? Do I know anyone in the countryside? Damnit. I barely have any food or water supplies. I'm not prepared for this.*

I ran off the bus the moment the doors opened at my stop, hardly looking as I crossed the street. The dogs barked as I inserted the key and opened the door. They jumped on me as I entered the apartment, nearly knocking me over.

'Okay guys, I need you to behave. We're about to get into a situation.' Smart as ever, the two of them stepped back to give me space to enter the bedroom.

Backpack. I need a backpack. I snatched my blue school bag off the floor. This would have to do.

Okay, what do I need first? As if on cue, Fred and George whined. Right, dog food. I grabbed the container and threw it in. Great, it already took half the space. I moved to the kitchen. Granola bars, canned veggies . . . I did not have a lot of long-lasting food. I looked at the bread and laughed. Bread was always the first thing to go when extreme weather was forecasted. *Will it be the same now?* Bloody hell, I wasn't prepared for this.

My hands shook and I dashed to the bathroom. *Hygiene products? Basic hygiene is important, right?* Without it, that's how people got sick. Face wipes. Dry shampoo. Toothpaste. Fred poked his head around the corner of the bathroom, rope toy in mouth. He looked at me expectantly.

'No Fred, there's no time for that!'

As if in protest upon hearing my words, George bounded around the corner, carrying three tennis balls in his mouth. Giant dog that he was, he was unable to stop his momentum and crashed into the side of the tub. There was a distinct crack as the plastic siding covering the length of the tub broke and fell away.

'Damnit, George!'

He dropped the tennis balls and flattened himself against the floor, putting his ears back. Guilty by association, Fred joined him.

'What happened?' My flatmates asked coming to stand on either side of the doorway in the bathroom. 'Holy shit!'

I looked back to see what had caught their attention and my mouth dropped open. With the plastic siding fallen, the true nature of the tub was revealed.

'Talk about toxic . . . that's why we keep getting sick,' one of my flatmates commented.

Covering the entire side of the tub, was a large, fuzzy wall of mould. I dropped my backpack and sat on the floor. Crazy landlady. Blaming her allergies and sickness on the dogs every time she popped around unannounced.

Mould. Just a wall of mould. And the winter flu season.

So not a zombie apocalypse after all...

(8, 119)

Plan for the You To-Do Tomorrow
Amanda-Marie Kale

4:32 AM	Enter last cycle of REM sleep
5:18 AM	Dream about that one crush from three years ago and you're running on a sidewalk being chased by quicksand, bed falling –
5:19 AM	Wake up and pee.
5:23 AM	Go back to bed, please. Must write by 7 AM.
5:48 AM	Go back to bed, please. Must write by 7 AM.
6:21 AM	Go back to bed, please. Must write –

6:25 AM   Eat breakfast:

                              Coffee, black. Three seconds sprinkled sugar. The brown kind.

                              Large-seeded toast.
                              Natural PB.
                              Lather it up.

                              Banana.
                              Most bruised, eat first.

6:50 AM   Set up:

                              Five pillows

                              Laptop. Netflix.

                              Gilmore Girls paused at beginning of season 2 episode – ooooh, this is the one with the –

8:30 AM   Peel outta bed mid-stream cause Stars Hollow will never exist for you, you will never be them you will never have their perfectly scripted balance, not when you're acting like this you little –

                        Clean dishes.

8:40 AM	Wash face twice and lotion.
8:41 AM	Stretch, yoga, half-hearted.
8:41 AM	Dress yourself in comfy clothes that are aesthetically pleasing
8:55 AM	Change your mind 'cause you're doing laundry today not Sunday –
9:01 AM	Focus! Look, there's your library books.
9:02 AM	Look, your favourite books by your nightstand.
9:03 AM	Look, those stacks of books nicely framed by your reading chair.

9:04 AM	Effectively decide not to read any of them and then proceed to complain, *help you help you why can't you write* in this lamentable chorus to that heaven in your ceiling 'cause this ephemeral little 'gift' isn't easy enough for you, isn't it???
10:30 AM	Get off emails and social media and Facebook – aren't you against this???
10:30 AM	All right, calm down. Breathe. I'm here for you.
	Fresh air. That's just what you need. Fresh air. Go on a walk. Just go. Get out. Gotta get that blood flowing –
11:11 AM	Slam door drop big sleeping-bag puffer and *oh, woe is you!*
	Bemoan – howl – *weep* over lack of sunlight or happiness or joy.
	Wail – *bewail* the country so lacking in your home-ness, your home, your sequestered home for the next twelve months and NOW:

11:12 AM	Enter the sweet embrace of your daily existential crisis, your one true lover and the most passionate affair you've had to date.
11:15 AM	Let it coo and woo you beneath the covers.
11:18 AM	Let it stretch and snuggle and moan around your curled toes.
11:20 AM	Let it slap you silly, slap you silly kid those tears are weak.
11:30 AM	You're weak.
11:40 AM	You're a fucking child, aren't you?
11:50 AM	What don't you have?
11:50 AM	I said WHAT DON'T YOU FUCKING HAVE.

11:58 AM   No no no no don't look up you don't get to blame God this time.

11:59 AM   You did this, to yourself.

4:32 PM   Sundown is much too early.

Arise to a Spotify playlist you've titled 'Enjoy' and *la da di* decide you're gonna take charge of your life *la da day* you're gonna sticky-note a future that is distracted *la da da* that is devoid *la da di* that is innocently forgetful of human interaction or career passions because *tra la la* it's just another long to-do in a crossed-off scratch of *la di fucking da* and you sing *hum diddly doo* to your cheap world-map tapestry:

Where can I be satisfied?

(3, 31)

I Don't Think I Can Be Your Writer Anymore
Amanda-Marie Kale

I don't think I can be your writer anymore because I like pretending I'm happy.

I sit in nostalgia and vomit keys into word processors and it gives me a sort of high I can't describe (like a writer could). But then again, so does putting on clean new clothes and stepping out of myself and breathing in . . . *what's the word?*

I don't think you can be a writer anymore because I don't like your style. Or what you have to say. I don't like your bits and pieces, and I don't like the way you don't like me. Like my writing. Like me. What the fuck do you know anyway?

(I think I like pretending I'm happy more so than being happy because *being* happy is a lifelong commitment to something else I can't grasp. Sure I'm passionate about my dark cloud but there's a sweetness in the panic attacks that push me to be happier.) So I don't think I can be your writer anymore.

((Because the cloud doesn't hang above respectfully like it's drawn for Charlie fucking Brown it fucking hugs you in its density. No, not 'hug' . . . *what's the word?* Less than 'consumption,' but stronger than 'touch.' And I really don't like being touched. Not unless I've decided I like it. When you see me and think you can stroke my shoulder-blades or squeeze my shoulders, *who the fuck* you don't know me.))

I don't think I can be your writer anymore because I liked being fucked, okay? I like it I like it I like it and when I like it I think about it a *lot* because we fuck in my writing space and I stare at the bed and I sleep in late and think of it all in vapor, arms locking behind my back because no amount of closeness is close enough to heal. Because, okay. Because it feels good. Because I can. Because I'm young and writing is for the birds. Writing is for the old.

What?

I don't think I can be your writer anymore because when I'm sad all I ever have are one-night stands it doesn't fuel me to write anything. I can only write about the distant past and that past isn't even past but it's most definitely passed. I don't think I can write when I'm this shallow.

(Oh my god you're judging me for being this shallow.) ((I can't do this anymore.))

I don't think I can be an author when I'm *older and wiser* because my ideas are kitchen sinks. I love nothing-more than multiplying dirty dishes and nobody likes to clean a dirty dish. Hey, that wasn't half bad?

Yes, it was.

I don't think you can be my reader anymore because no matter how many times you ask me where I'm from I can never give you the perfect answer. Yes, you do want perfection. Yes, I do want you to know me. Want them, to know us. Know us in a way that doesn't raise questions? Know us as a smart intelligent mysterious authoress – with an alluring yet unrelatable backstory – all while . . . *what's the word?*

No, I really don't want you to be my reader anymore, okay? You heard me. You always think I'm stupid, and I have an irrational fear of them all THEM ALL exposing me just like you and laughing at my naked moles and appendix scars until they spot my un-education. Is that why I'm a student again? Is that . . . *where is the right word?*

I don't think I can be your writer anymore because I'm not stupid and I never was. I'm highly employable. I'm spectacularly unbalanced. I've always known exactly what you were doing. I'm wholly responsible for me, for us. Both sides, both faces, both brains, both bodies and fingers and blinking eyes.

Because we did this, to ourselves.

I don't think I can be your writer anymore because I never really was to begin with, was I?

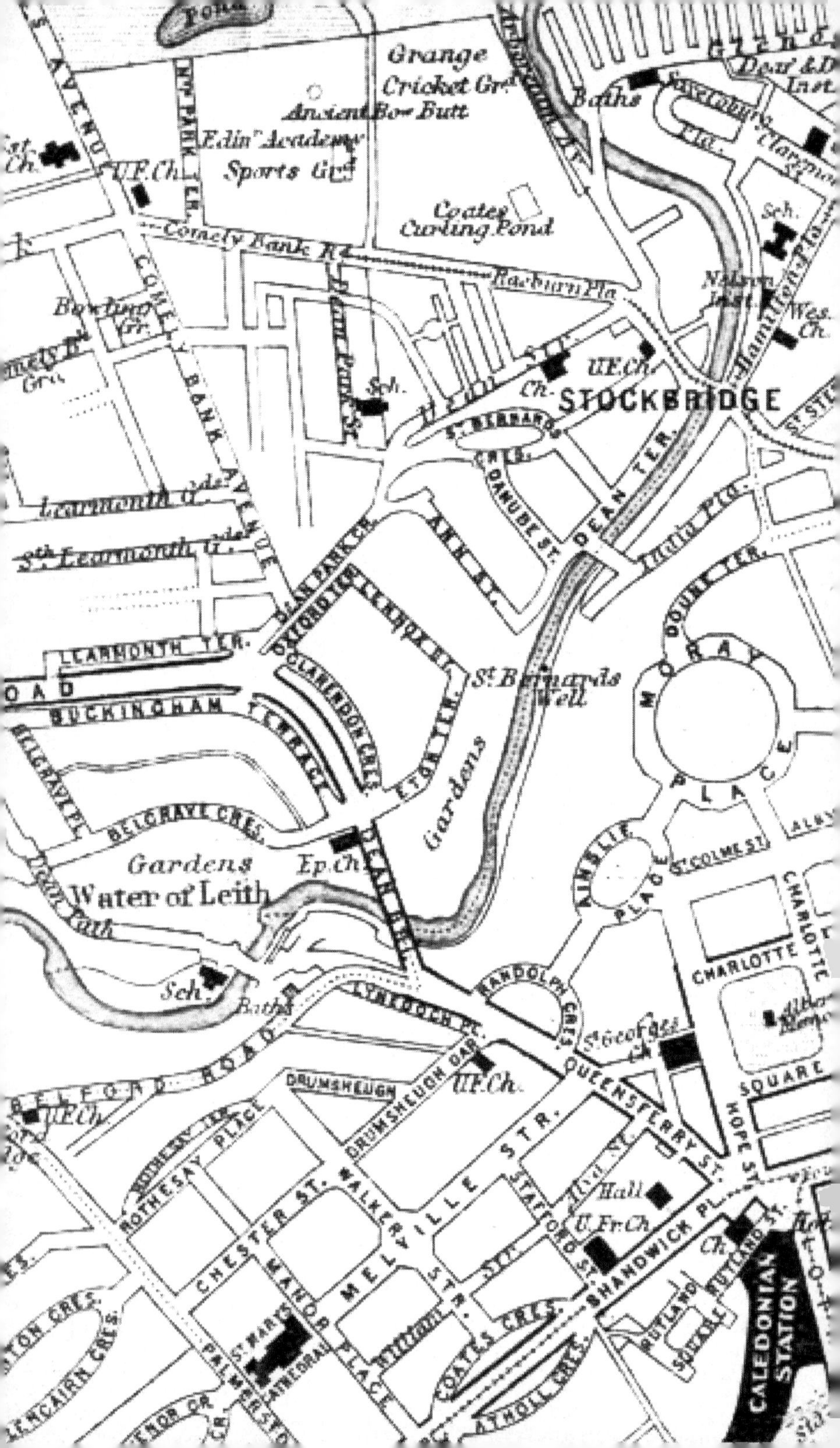

Grange Cricket Grd.
Ancient Bow Butt
Edin'r Academy Sports Grd.
Coates Curling Pond
Comely Bank Rd.
Raeburn Pl.
Baths
U.F.Ch.
Bowling Gr.
Sch.
STOCKBRIDGE
St. Bernards Cres.
Danube St.
Dean Ter.
Ann St.
India Pl.
Doune Ter.
Moray Place
Learmonth Ter.
Buckingham Terrace
Clarendon Cres.
Oxford Ter.
Lennox St.
Eton Ter.
St. Bernards Well
Gardens
Belgrave Cres.
Ep. Ch.
Water of Leith
Ainslie Place
St. Colme St.
Charlotte
Randolph Cres.
Lynedoch Pl.
Queensferry St.
Belford Road
Drumsheugh
Drumsheugh Gdns.
Rothesay Place
Chester St.
Walker St.
Melville Str.
Stafford St.
Hall
U. Fr. Ch.
Shandwick Pl.
Hope St.
Rutland St.
Rutland Square
Coates Cres.
Atholl Cres.
Manor Place
Palmerston Pl.
Caledonian Station
St. Mary's Cathedral
Square

EXCERPTS

Mint Castle
John Reid

Prologue

The frenzy of the crowd engulfed the courtyard. Head clamped in the stocks and forced downward, the expression of the accused was hidden by her rancid, tangled hair, but one could imagine a face contorted by agony and injustice. The peasants directly in front of the platform were wide-eyed, with teeth bared, a churning mass made real in the glare of the sun. They hurled all manner of rotten things, tomatoes, fish heads, which splattered off her bruised fingers, the crown of her head, and the front of her thin, bloodied legs.

Two days. That's what's written down. For two days, she was forced to endure this living hell, without relief, her own filth gathering around her naked feet. That was until, of course, on the third day, the delegate returned to the village, the prince among them, and in so doing brought her innocence to light. The jailer set her free, and with crooked limbs, she washed herself silently, before collecting her belongings. Then she disappeared into the forest, where she set about devising her revenge. But we'll pick it up from there next week.

Now just hold on a moment. Sit. Something peculiar has happened. I know that typically we struggle to cram the set material into the hours permitted to us each week, but turn to the clock. See there's time remaining. It's no illusion. You have a choice. We could glance at something we wouldn't normally look at, if you wanted, something not on the list. It's up to you. You can leave but I'd rather you stayed. I'll close my eyes.

Good. I'm happy you've stayed. Whenever you leave and I watch you from the window I can never quite tell if you're satisfied. But just knowing that you've stayed when you don't have to gives me confidence.

And fortunately I know what we should look at already, so without delay let us to turn to a man occupying a more, if you will, cobwebbed nook of Mint Castle's history, with regard to what you're used to. His name was Dalton. Almost definitely. And he was a fisherman. Before we proceed I must concede that we will struggle to start at Dalton's beginning, as there's none on record, however, from my own time spent researching the village I think I have managed to piece the fragments of his later life together, and seeing as you've stayed, God-bless you, should we encounter a blank I promise to only fill it with the most educated of estimations. Perhaps you won't even notice. Yes, I shall be as faithful as is possible to how I envision things must have been.

Now Dalton was most certainly married, and though I know very little about his wife, I do know that she drowned in the river. That said, I would like very much to tiptoe over this tragedy because it doesn't seem to bear any relevance to what I want to talk about. Perhaps I should be letting you make these decisions. No, I'm conscious of time, and I feel all that would only get in the way of what *is* worth exploring, which is, and keep in mind that this is the sort of unsubstantiated, indefinite, word-of-mouth tripe that I'm obliged to warn you against, I believe that Dalton may just have played a role in ending the famine that for a brief, historic moment brought the kingdom to its knees, the famine for which Barbantula was thought to be responsible. So that should keep you piqued, I hope. But yes, now we know better, of course. *Barbantula*, the infamous beast of the bay with her writhing, shadowy tentacles and her gleaming, vampiric fangs, that would have turned Vlad himself green, I'm sure, was not real. Though, as always, we must deny that false seniority that invariably creeps in with hindsight. Back in that time, in Dalton's time, she, Barbantula, absolutely and unequivocally *was* real. It was a different world then, almost. In any case, I'm curious to see what you make of it.

And we've been through everything else. That's the other reason, the secret reason, which I think it would be wrong to withhold, for inviting you to stay. I enjoy our time together, always, you know that, but it's history, isn't it? It's a finite resource. All the landmark stuff, the really pivotal stuff, the rebellions, the coups, the assassinations, the weddings, the links in the chain that make up the syllabus today, it's all been pillaged, done to death, I fear. We've done it to death and I'm worried that there's not much else to tell. That petrifies me, really. I think it would be the end of me, of us. That's what I'm worrying about whenever we sit here – well, I stand and you sit – and my voice drops like a stone to the floor.

Like here.

No doubt this is the wrong thing to say but that drop is just me tormenting myself – that's a strong word – but tormenting myself with the idea that I'm reducing what I'm saying by saying it, saddling you with repetition, repetition, repetition, repeating myself, my colleagues, something you've read – and also, I'm scared of what you think of me. I wonder, and yes, all this happens during that drop, I wonder if this is even educational at all. I'm sorry. I can't remember how we got here. I'm very old. You know it's strange, I can physically feel myself getting in the way now.

Enough. Time to let it breathe. My aim for the next short while is for you to forget that I'm here. I cannot believe how long this monologue has gone on for. Nothing drove me further to despair when I was in your position, let's say forty or fifty years ago, in this room, no less, these walls, these books, these desks, these chairs, that door – they haven't redecorated, by the way – and a rambling, hard-to-follow monologue was thrust upon me by some rickety old creature. It was terrible, and I remember thinking there and then, sitting where you're sitting, that if I'm ever so lucky as to find myself in that position up there, that's not how I'm going to do it. So we'll maybe pause about halfway for refreshment and brief discussion, if the clock is kind, say around the incident in the market, which certainly happened, that I do know for sure.

But please, allow me to re-emphasise that this is not history designed to be told. In fact, let's not even call it history, history is for things written in ink or carved into stone. Let's call this, I don't know, an educated approximation of the past, no, that's too close to history, we'll decide on something later. You'll see what I mean for yourself, I suppose, as unlike everything else we study there'll be no epiphany at the end, in truth, as with Dalton's beginning there is no end. None I trust, at least, none that seems right. A part of me feels a little ashamed about this already, and would even consider offering you one final opportunity to leave and go home to your family and sit down with them and tell them over dinner that well, it was just an everyday sort of day, to be honest, the sun came up and then it went down, but there's not enough time.

So this is what happened. We won't try and put a date on it, but I'll start with him waist-deep in the river, rod in hand and leaning back against the current, just a few moments before he went blind.

(1, 105)

A Dance With The Devil
Kirsty Souter

I've heard my rev'rend graunie say,
In lanely glens ye like to stray;– ROBERT BURNS

Nothing brought the toun together like pretending to be shocked that Jeanie Macgregor had been caught in a compromising situation with the mason's apprentice. The pair were quite the spectacle, red faced and red-eyed; perched on high, uncomfortable stools in front of the congregation of family and neighbours.

Malcolm stared at the scene, gooseflesh prickling under his sleeves. He wasn't convinced it was because of the draught that was blowing in through the boarded-up gaps where the windows used to be. He wanted to relax his shoulders but feared the pew might bite him if he leant back too far.

Those that covereth sins . . . shall not prosper . . .

It would have been too easy to follow the example of his mother – and all the other auld biddies of the parish – and stare at the two offenders with quiet tuts of disapproval until the kirk session was over. Instead, Malcolm trained his eyes on the minister. Morton was a figure to behold. His tall frame rose up from billowing black robes, stately and eagle nosed. He was a fairly young man, not much older than Malcolm, but he was learned. He knew how to brandish doctrine in a way that curled toes inside the boots of even the toughest old farmer.

But whoso confesses . . . forsaketh them . . .

The minister thumped the pulpit, spit flying from his mouth. *Would the two sinners renounce their behaviour?* He recalled how such immorality provoked God's fury; of the lean years He had wrought. Did their peers have anything to hide? His sharp eyes scanned the faces before him, his accusing finger drawing a shiver across the room. Would the gathered join together and pray the Lord forgive these miscreants, and all others who might follow their example? Malcolm clasped his hands together and bowed his head with the others. Consternation and coin were both mighty prices to pay, and Malcolm didn't know which he feared most. More and more of his neighbours found themselves sitting before the parish on those high stools every passing week. Their sins were on full display in front of *Heaven's unblinking gaze* and, most pressingly, the toun's. Whatever the smashing of the kirk's stained glass windows had begun, Minister Morton's arrival finished. His austere glare and Edinburgh turn of phrase served as a constant reminder that life was changing.

The door in the back of the church creaked open.

People shuffled, and a clatter of footsteps announced a crowd of late arrivals. The minister raised his voice. Opening one eye and tilting in the pew, Malcolm could just about make out the troupe that trekked in to fill the ranks. They huddled together at the edge of the room, whispering amongst themselves and craning to watch the minister's tirade. The strangers – well. Were they really *strangers*? They had been here for some time now, near a month, by his reckoning. They were here for the harvest. Malcolm had seen them in the fields; strange, half shod creatures, plaid wraps and broad frames. His thoughts were cut short by a jab from his mother's elbow. She'd some nerve; she could barely stop herself from vibrating with all the gossip she was looking forward to dissecting after the sermon. He shifted back to the front. *Amen.*

—

The church rose out of the glen, every bit as imposing as the hills that surrounded it. The buildings of the fermtoun seemed to spill out in its wake, like a cluster of panicked ducklings trying to catch up to their mother. The late midsummer sun cast long shadows across the peaty soil, twisting and turning around low dykes and fertile run-rigs. Squat and grey, the church sat unflinching. Every Sabbath day, the denizens of the parish would put down their tools and set aside their work, to trickle through its doors, filling the rough wooden pews; turning their attention heavenward.

Malcolm felt a huge weight lifting from his shoulders when the session was dismissed and they were finally allowed to escape from the cold stone building. His legs ached from inactivity. He could hardly wait to head back home. The wind was bracing, and brought with it the scent of the peat and clover. Malcolm's eyes were drawn to the strange folk again. Strange family, he supposed. They had a shared appearance, dark hair and sharp, pale features. They huddled together, away from the congregation, near the drystone wall that surrounded the kirk. Jeanie Macgregor would thank her stars that they had chosen this, of all days, to observe the session.

Can ye believe that they'd the nerve tae jist barge in like that?

Whit a gas, did ye see the face on – Oh! Braw sermon, Meenister Morton!

The wagging tongues that stood around in the kirkyard – leaning upon gravestones and glancing furtively at each other – had very active imaginations, and a more than generous helping of moral indignation. Jeanie Macgregor, walking scandal though she was, had left very little to inspire the imagination. They would remember Jeanie tomorrow; but for now, there were a gaggle of oddities to deal with.

Haven't ever seen the hale gang o' them in the kirk

at once afore, bairns an' aw!

Aye well, can ye blame 'em? It's gey draughty wi'oot the windaes . . .

A strange pit twisted in the bottom of Malcolm's stomach as the family turned to leave, hopping the wall instead of taking the main path through the kirk yard.

One of the women – a daughter, perhaps? – twisted, glared into the crowd. He studied her face, angular and drawn, with just a hint of sun blush on the end of her nose. Her peat-coloured hair was stuffed haphazardly into a threadbare coif. Their eyes met.

Minister Morton must hae threatened them intae it, comin' all at once . . .

Noo, wouldn't ye know

The fire in her dark eyes made him blink and turn away, blushing. Had he really been staring? He felt her eyes boring through the back of his skull as he jammed his hands into the pockets of his overcoat and strode away from the kirk in the opposite direction.

'Malcolm! Malcolm!' the cry came from behind him, 'Where're ye gaun?'

'Ma, I'm auld enough tae be walkin' home by ma-sel',' he shouted back, 'I ken where we live.'

'Ach, will ye no slow down and let yer auld mither catch ye up?'

Huffing like an overweight sow, his mother barrelled up behind him. She grabbed his arm, wheezing.

'Crivvens, Ma, whit are ye daein'?' Malcolm stopped dead, letting her catch her breath. 'Ye sound fit tae drop, ye ken fine the doctor said ye're no supposed tae –'

'Ach, well, ah didnae ken why ye were gaun aff like someone had set yer trews oan fire! Ye could hae stopped!' she looked at him accusingly, grasping at her sides.

'I didnae want tae interrupt –' Malcolm stifled a shudder as he saw those dark, accusing eyes again.

'Ye didnae want tae talk about the Lammas festival mair like! Dinnae think ah didnae notice when ye took aff!'

With his mother hanging onto his arm, Malcolm began to walk again, picking his way along the pebble track that ran through the fermtoun.

'The Lammas?'

'Ach, dinnae try and pretend, ah ken whit ye young'uns are like!' his mother chuckled, squeezing his arm. 'Why, it was Lammas Eve when yer faither, God rest his soul –'

'I thought the minister telt us yon 'heathen practises' were fer Catholics and teuchters, and that we're tae have nae part in them.'

She snorted. Without looking, Malcolm knew she was making the face she made whenever he walked in the door after spreading manure. 'Yon meenister! Ah dinnae ken wha died and left him in charge!'

'The last minister, Ma,' Malcolm said, followed by an exclamation as she aimed a skelp at the back of his head.

'Ye ken whit ah mean! Ach, it's too bad. Ah cannae keep up wi' all this kirk business at aw!' She paused in what Malcolm could only assume was a moment of uncharacteristically sombre reflection.

'Aye, well,' Malcolm tried to picture how it would feel, perched up at the front of the church. 'My coffers and my guid name are inclined tae dae what he says!'

'Nivver ye heed yer coffers, ye should be concerned wi' yer immortal soul!' his mother replied.

'Aye, some bugger micht tell that tae Minister Morton!'

'Malcolm, ye cannae go around talkin' like that!' his mother chided. 'But . . . ach, well, it's no as if ye cannae still uphold *some* traditions . . . '

'Ma! I'm no proposin' a trial marriage tae anyone fer the Lammas! Besides, it's harvest time!'

'Noo, ye listen tae yer mither!'

'Chrissakes –'

'Yer no gettin' oany younger, son. Noo, yer faither, God –'

'God rest his soul, *aye*, I ken!'

'*God rest his soul*, yer faither and I were married younger'n you, and God willin' we'd still be married noo if it wisnae fer the lang winter! Ah jist want ye tae be –'

Malcolm had been having the same conversation with his mother ever since he'd come of age. He'd tried to make her see it his way, but he would have had more success trying to teach the sheep to bring themselves down off the hill in the winter. 'Ma, I'll be happy when I can afford ma ain land and I dinnae hae tae fight the bluidy teuchters fer work during the harvest!'

'Malcolm –' she began, in a wheedling voice.

'If yer goin' tae be like this, auld woman, I'll let ye walk yersel' home!' Malcolm said, but he was laughing.

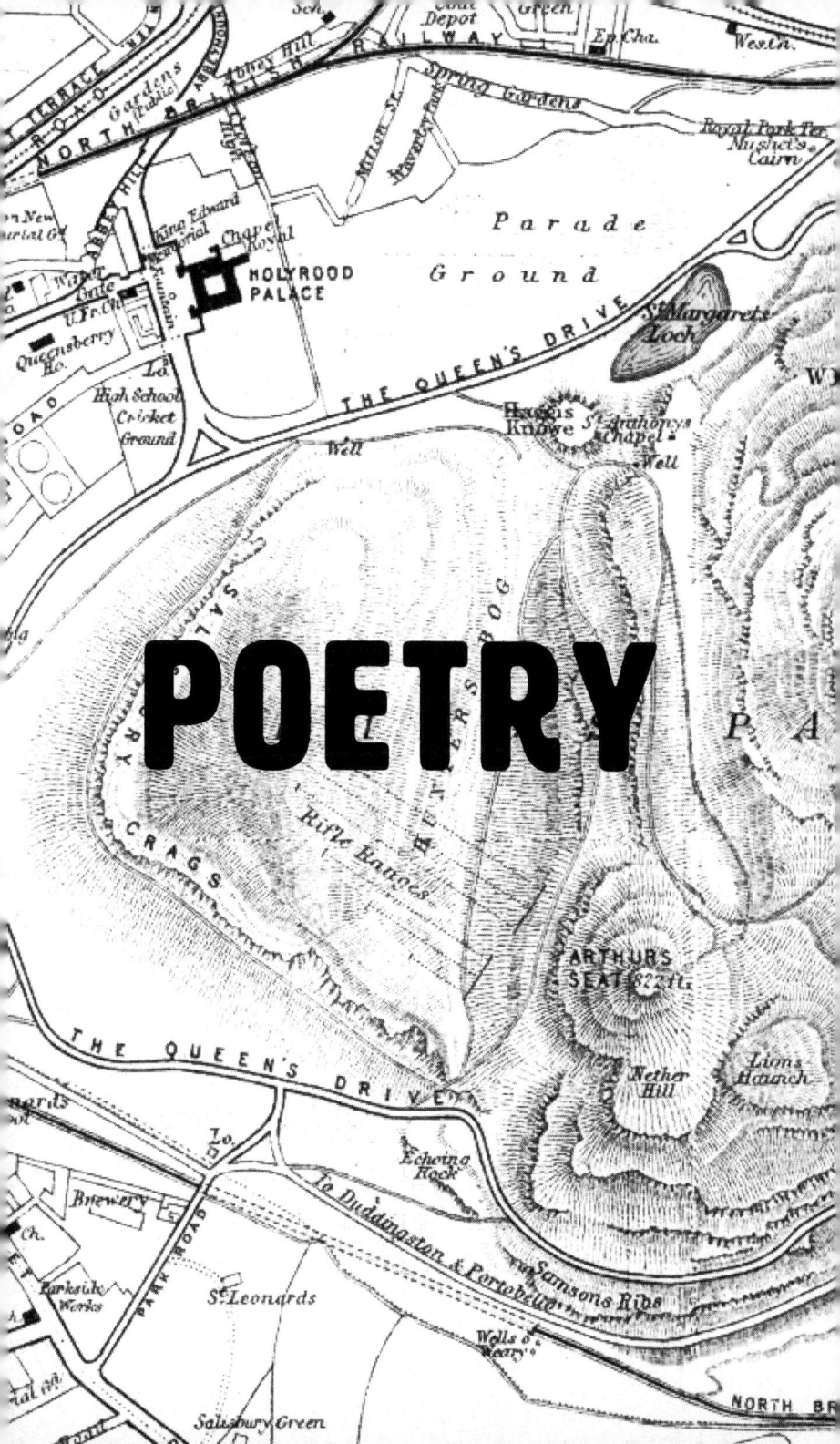

To Edinburgh With Love
Ning Cai

your slopes, your sublime slopes
flowing like water, like secrets
never before heard, I tremble
as I taste your sloe berries
luscious against all senses
music
soft bubbling of your river: leith
hidden in the wildness of ravelston woods
your reality feeding me
your voracious appetite
for life
the width
and depth
and length of it
longing for tactile
seasons
of desire
deliciously bound
by craving
your hills and
lascivious paths
tracing the promise

of pleasure
in a body so small
yet so full of talent
embracing the rhythm of portobello's tides, tireless
passion crackles, embers glow
your voice scottish wildcat
words that capture my heart
rake memories down my willing skin
play with my restless fingers
your stories, your invitations
i am powerless against your charms:
unstoppable force
you rename my sky, my stars, my moon and make me

yours

(2,17)

Secret Base
Dexter Yim

Inside this mahogany box,
only some origami paper
with our names on it;
the box is always a backdrop
to my memories.

He loved to play Super Sentai,
She loved to play Sailor Moon,
I loved to play Kamen Rider.
We shared the same dream
of protecting The World;
memories crumple these costumes.

I am like a vagrant spider
weaving invisible webs to
catch you both, to return you
to our secret base where
we see the crack of dawn, the close of day;
forgotten but not gone.

(2, 135)

Kintsugi
Dexter Yim

Strong in broken places,
embracing damage,
joining fragments.

To *kintsugi* the rupture
is like tying the wound
with a ligature,

or like not knowing
you are crying when tears
spill down your sweat-drenched face,

or like telling the difference
between your dark skin
and a sun-kissed back.

Cracks are like shadows
searching for the light –
broken perfection.

(7, 143)

Murphy's Law
Dexter Yim

To my teacher Melody Law and her family
'Anything that can go wrong will go wrong'

Daddy, every time the toast
lands butter-side down,
You pick it up and laugh –

The necklace and earrings
you buy in an upmarket store
are fake but I cherish them –

The hawthorn berries
are ripe enough
yet they taste sour –

The beach near our cabin
has too much shingle
but not enough sand –

                                        I know, my daughter,

You are not like a bird
alighting on the branch,
flying away –

You always bitterly complain
the school uniforms I bought
are either too big or too small –

You don't like mallards,
only their iridescent feathers;
ambivalent, veracious –

To our saffron memories:
whatever can happen will happen!

(10,129)

Museum of Childhood
Ellie Jackson

Welcome

take out your treasure chest,

rebuild the trinkets,

tack them together

with bubble-gum.

The Original Folk and Fairy Tales of the Brother's Grimm, First Edition, 1812

the lost corners of paper snowflakes

melt on your tongue.

Polly Pocket Cruise Ship, 1998

a kitsch castle,

coral cladding renders

it too heavy to be

classed as a castle in the air,

too heavy

to hold in your hands.

Victorian Doll House, 1853

a stroll down doll house lane,
the tea tables and oil lamps
are thrown out
leaving space
for your imagination to install
whimsical waterslides.

Display of Dolls, 1821-present

swallowed into
the womb of a colossal Russian doll,
you burrow through face after face,
and reach a displaced head
stuffed with a lightbulb:
the smallest doll is the blush of a night light.

Thank you and Goodbye

on your way out
the plastic phone goes
ring ring, ring a ring a rosie
like the pressure of blood in your ears.

(6, 50)

speckled brains
Ellie Jackson

in the kitchen

I crack speckled brains

against the rim of a glass bowl;

the yolks of silent head-screams

slip out.

a little lingers on my fingers,

crusts around my nails;

I want to scrape it off,

but the knife has sunk

deep into another dimension,

beneath the beetroot juice

and moon-spots of cheese

bruises land

on my skin, like moths,

as I click open the clasps

of Pandora's Tupperware box.

(4, 98)

sunday afternoon
Ellie Jackson

outside, a telephone wire,

heartbeat monitor,

electric-shocking

the sky

inside, the freckled

window frame,

a pin-head

is mistaken

for a ladybird

eyelashes lend

not-there wings

a beat

but she still can't decide

if her laundry is damp

or just cold

against the bank, asleep
Stefano Paparo

on some newspapers, a woman

in a red winter coat

has made a pillow

of her forearms.

nearby, as if pushed

under the foot

of an invisible bed, her

empty black shoes.

asteroid
Stefano Paparo

even the weatherman cries

when he hears the song –

the deep synth

of that astral whale

trolling for a fuck.

what got me
Stefano Paparo

was the fog.

a low cloud

getting sick

in the hollow

of a dead god.

it's a different

kind of science

but it's true.

that cloud was

drunk, inappropriate

ly shaped, tired

nearly extinct.

like many things

on earth

that cloud

had attained

enough

mass

to become

an embarrassment:

liopleurodon

atmosphere

honeybee – forgotten

names on the breath

of a demented

sun.

(4, 40)

Fledgling
Elspeth Reilly

this morning I nearly stepped on a bird
that, dazed and scared, stood shaking
its tiny beak agape, pink sliver of a tongue
tasting the wind that slithers
between the gaps in my fence

at this pub everyone
could be my grandparents:
shivery hands,
finicky orders,
and winter coats still on
though it's really quite warm in here:
warm like a soft bird body
scooped up and nestled in
a plant pot to rest

I tuck myself into a corner
after playing pick-a-pint roulette,
and I lose: it stales in the mouth

in front of me, two ladies are swallowed
by the fading upholstery of their booth
the loud one berates the other who sits small
with her hat all askew on her head

well you should call her then, shouldn't you?
sneering through a mouth of burger, no bun,
as the fork scrapes mustard off the plate
you're the one that gets lonely
laughing and straightening her back
stiff like the stairwell railings
that trail upstairs to her right

the small woman scrunches
her soft bluish body and face
oh yes, well, I do in the evenings sometimes

and I quiver around the lip
of the pint glass, swallow,
pinching the bar napkin
into a pile of wet red shreds

the plant pot is empty when I return home
and settled in trees, countless birds
I watch their polka-dot bodies
before it all blurs

Soap Lady
Elspeth Reilly

Mütter Museum, Philadelphia

bat-nosed and screaming
her lower teeth unhinged
upon a missing tongue

cream-yellow specks
on a blackened body
caked thick with grave wax

exhumed from her coffin
once bedded in wormy soil
she stretches

in a finger-smudged
glassy casket –
hollow eyed

watches dead flies
in fluorescent lights
behind gawking faces

in flushed-faced youth
did the white linens, still wet
from the bucket, whip in the wind

and cling against the curves of her body
with the smell of lye lingering on skin,
her fingers red-raw from the washboard?

(1, 162)

The Usual
Elspeth Reilly

red crackling of upholstered stools
tired from the wet weight of rainy men
who mumble to no one about the weather

ordering drinks as stiff
as the brim of their hats
that sit, drying, besides muddy boots

scattered along the rough grain of the bar
candles flicker and light filters
through spotty tumblers held by shaking hands

a slow drip of wax hangs low and pools,
and idle fingers press and imprint
those glossy white coins, warm to the touch

like loose change stored in a front pocket,
close to the quickening beat of a heart
slow-soaked in sloe gin and tonic

the sun wavers through warped glass,
borrowed light, catching and holding
the dimly lit faces of daytime drunks

when ice clinks in empty drinks
they pay with fat hands of dimes
that clatter and dance with hard taps

leaving only when the waxy moon
sits high in foggy sky, and the rain
dappled roads have begun to dry

the chairs stand taller in the empty,
the wax is scraped, the wicks are wetted,
tumblers soaped, dried, and stacked

the shutters cover window panes
leaving only pinstripes of light
and forgotten jackets

(9, 24)

Our Garden of Love
Ali Musa Ame

I wish there were a portal
to send me back to the time
we met in the garden of roses:
you would embrace me tight
like a baby in her mother's arms,
while I sipped honey
from your wet lips.

I long for the touch of henna tattoos on your back;
I yearn for the soft caress of your round breasts;
I crave for the sobs in the midst of pleasant pain
mixed with squeaks of a clapping bed.

And though days trudge like weeks,
Weeks crawl like months,
Months trek like years,
Hopes droop and wither,
and promises take forever:
I will always dream
Of seeing you again.

(2, 83)

Unyago[1] Song
Ali Musa Ame

Cry not, cry not, my little child
Sing and dance, don't be shy;
Roll your eyes with a female pride;
Soon you'll become someone's bride.

Wipe your kitchen clean and dry
Harvest the banana while it's ripe
Take the calabash, put it inside
The best time for cooking is at night

Watch and learn, my little child
Wear your *khanga*[1] when you leave the hut
Snakes will waylay you outside
Guard your ring, don't let them bite.

---

1 Unyago: An initiation ceremony for preparing young girls to woman hood.

2 Khanga: Women's cultural clothing in Zanzibar

The Lion in the Royal Emblem
Ali Musa Ame

Handcuffed and in pain,
he looks at the royal emblem
in the detention centre
and the golden lion smiles at him,
showing how great the country is.

He is in a dark cell
waiting to be removed
back to the land of the Kilimanjaro
because his papers have expired,
or so he was told.

Maybe if the golden lion
had not been in Africa
taking the lion's share
and plundering its wealth,

maybe, just maybe,
no blacks would be in handcuffs
while the golden lion
in the royal emblem
smiles at them;
forcing them to return to countries
she once created.

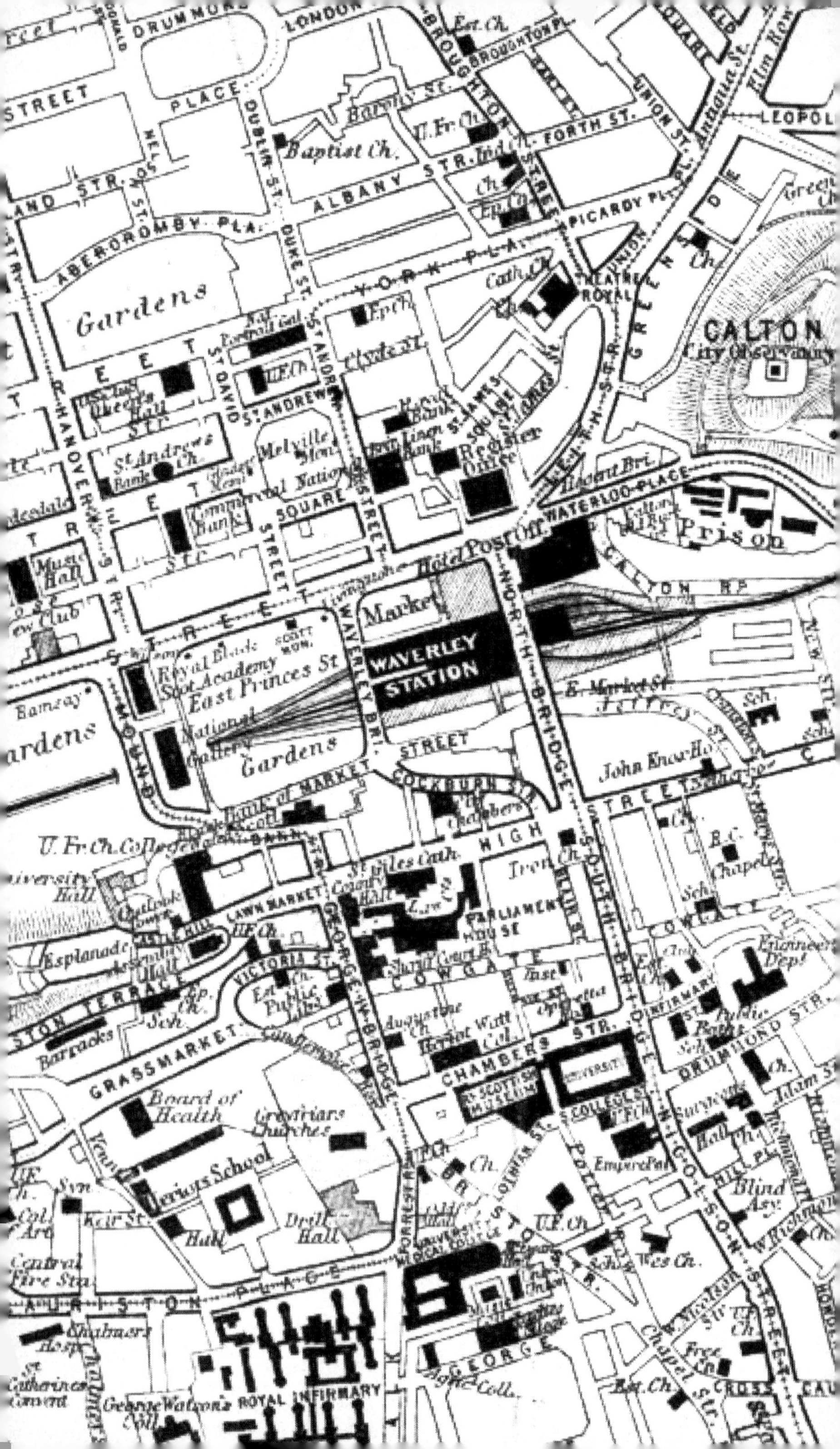

DRUMMOND
LONDON
BROUGHTON PL.
STREET
PLACE
DUBLIN ST.
Baptist Ch.
ALBANY STR.
FORTH ST.
UNION ST.
LEOPOLD
ABERCROMBY PLA.
DUKE ST.
PICARDY PL.
YORK PLA.
Gardens
Cath. Ch.
THEATRE ROYAL
CALTON
City Observatory
ST. DAVID
ST. ANDREW ST.
Clyde St.
ST. ANDREW SQ.
Melville Mon.
Royal Bank
Register Office
HANOVER ST.
St. Andrew's Ch.
Commercial Bank
SQUARE
WATERLOO PLACE
Regent Bri.
Post Off.
Prison
Music Hall
Hotel
Market
WAVERLEY STATION
NORTH BRIDGE
CALTON RD.
Royal Scot. Academy
East Princes St.
Gardens
National Gallery
Scott Mon.
E. Market St.
Jeffrey St.
Ramsay
Gardens
WAVERLEY BRI.
COCKBURN STR.
MARKET
John Knox Ho.
HIGH STREET
St. Giles Cath.
Tron Ch.
BLAIR ST.
R.C. Chapel
U. Fr. Ch. College
University Hall
Outlook Tower
LAWN MARKET
PARLIAMENT HOUSE
COWGATE
Esplanade
Assembly Hall
VICTORIA ST.
GEORGE IV BRIDGE
Public Library
SOUTH BRIDGE
INFIRMARY ST.
Engineers Dept.
TERRACE
Barracks
GRASSMARKET
Heriot Watt Col.
CHAMBERS STR.
UNIVERSITY
DRUMMOND STR.
Board of Health
Greyfriars Churches
Heriot's School
Surgeons Hall
Blind Asy.
Drill Hall
FORREST RD.
U.F. Ch.
Wes. Ch.
UNIVERSITY MEDICAL SCHOOL
Central Fire Sta.
LAURISTON PLACE
Chalmers Hosp.
St. Catherines Convent
George Watson's Coll.
ROYAL INFIRMARY
GEORGE SQ.
NICOLSON STREET
Chapel Str.
CROSS
Est. Ch.
Free Ch.

PRIZEWINNERS

Sloan Prize 2019

The Sloan Prize is awarded annually for a prose or verse composition in Lowland Scots vernacular to a matriculated student or to a graduate of the University of Edinburgh of less than three years' standing.

Charles Lang

Charles Lang is from Castlemilk in Glasgow. He is a recent graduate from the University of Edinburgh, and is currently studying at the Seamus Heaney Centre in Belfast.

Clairvoyant
Charles Lang

I didny really wanty go but wee Louise in the work wis huvin people roon for her 30th. I says Louise I'll come roon n huv a few drinks wae yees n that but I'm no wantin a readin. The last hing I wanted wis tae waste ma last £30 fur a doollaly bastard tae tell me ma granny wis whisperin nice wee hings in his ear. Or so I thought. So we're huvin a few drinks n as soon as he comes in he clocks me right away n says aw hen you're no wantin a readin ur ye n I'm sittin there thinkin how the fuck dae you know. Naw I says I don't think so n the guy's right starin it me n says are ye sure? Anywiy we're aw sittin talkin away n people ur up n doon n gon ben fur readins n comin back n givin is aw the shite aboot he knew I hud three weans how did he know I hud three weans n I'm thinkin nae wonder Theresa ye plaster it aw er Facebook. Then Susan comes back in greetin cos the guy wis sayin her wee ma wis talkin tae her sayin keep the chin up hen I'll always be there fur ye n I was thinkin aye right. But it wis a pure sin cos her wee ma's no that long passed away. Anywiy wanst everybody's hud their turn we're aw sittin n the guy comes ben n says ur ye sure yer no wantin a readin hen I'll no even take nuthin aff ye fur it n the lassies ur lit Sharon you better go in he's got somebody fur ye he keeps askin so I thought fuck it n in I goes n sits doon n he says right I know ye wurny wantin a readin but I hud tae get ye in hen cos I've hud somebody here fur ye aw night. Honest tae God I couldny believe it.

Grierson Verse Prize 2019

The Grierson Verse Prize is awarded to a matriculated student of the University of Aberdeen or the University of Edinburgh for a composition in any recognized verse form except for 'free verse'.

Alycia Pirmohamed

Alycia Pirmohamed is a Ph.D. student at the University of Edinburgh, where she is studying the work of second-generation immigrant poets. She is the author of the chapbook Faces that Fled the Wind (forthcoming, BOAAT Press), and the winner of the 2018 Ploughshares Emerging Writers' Contest in poetry. Alycia received an M.F.A. from the University of Oregon.

Tritina for My India
Alycia Pirmohamed

Here is the seed of goodbye between myself & my India.
Here is the story of how I surrendered kutchi as a child.
Here are the ghosts of the great-greats I never knew:

In the reeds of Nangarpur Kutch, my great-grandfather knew
how to grow fruit on tough land, how to love his India.
He spoke the language of labourers, passed down to his child

the stones of stanzas without a written form & his child
passed down the aloed tongue to my father. Once, I too knew
the melodic fronds of this version of a version of an India—

an imagined India: the only homeland this child ever knew.

Lewis Edwards Memorial Award 2019

This prize was established in memory of Lewis Edwards, who died while a student of English Literature at the University. It is open to any matriculated undergraduate student of the University of Edinburgh.

Snigdha Koirala

Snigdha's work has previously appeared in *Lighthouse Literary Journal*, *Dirty Paws Poetry Review*, *Datableed*, and elsewhere. She is a student of literature at the University of Edinburgh.

Sunday Breakfast

Snigdha Koirala

Today,

I want to eat words.

Come over,

eat with me.

A yolk of poetry,

some tomatoes

from your garden.

Today,

I want your hands

kneading dough,

the sun slow

through the windows,

tipped from its jar.

Watch how it moves,

how it leads to a bowl

of oranges.

Last night I dreamed

of being opened like that,

read aloud

with no shame to bear.

Today,

you can peel back the rind

with your teeth.

Start from its navel,

unravel its scroll,

find within it

saps of gold, gleaming

like the shell of your ear.

There I'll trace salt

that rises,

humming seacoast,

sonorant.

Today,

I leave hunger

at the door.

I taste

in my natural

appetite

the bond

of live things

everywhere.

Eating pear

after pear,

down to the core,

then the core.

'I taste in my natural appetite the bond of lives things everywhere' is taken from Lucille Clifton's 'cutting greens.'

Map labels (Edinburgh — Holyrood / Salisbury Crags area)

- Prison
- Nelson's Mon!
- High School
- REGENT ROAD
- Calton New Burial G?
- Burns Mon!
- ABBEY HILL
- King Edward Memorial
- Chapel Royal
- HOLYROOD PALACE
- CALTON ROAD
- Whiteford Ho.
- Water Gate
- U. Fr. Ch.
- Fountain
- NEW ST
- Canongate Sch.
- Queensberry Ho.
- Tolbooth
- Sch.
- Lo.
- CANONGATE
- M:ray Ho.
- High School Cricket Ground
- St Tomb
- Training Coll.
- HOLYROOD ROAD
- B.C. Chapel
- Est. Ch.
- Sch.
- Engineers Dep?
- Arthur
- Bowling G?
- SALISBURY CRAGS
- DRUMMOND ST!
- Public Baths
- U. F. Ch.
- Quaker Cha.
- Arthur
- K
- Surgeons Hall
- Ch.
- Ph.
- Rifle
- Blind Asy.
- HILL
- Richmond St.
- Salisbury St
- ADAM ST
- ORANGE
- Brown St.
- Hosp.
- Carnegie
- Ch.
- U.F. Ch.
- Sch.
- NICOLSON
- RICHMOND ST.
- CROSS CAUSEWAY
- Free Ch.
- THE QUEEN'S D
- PLA.
- BUCCLEUCH
- U.F. Ch.
- St Leonards Coal Depot
- BARRELLOR ST
- Bowling Greens
- Est! Ch.
- HOPE
- MONTAGUE ST.
- ST LEONARDS STREET
- Lib?
- Brewery
- To
- Ch.
- PARK ROAD
- Hall
- U. F. Ch.
- Chapel Ter.
- St Peters Ep. Ch.
- Parkside Works
- St Leonards
- Royal (Dick) Veterinary Coll.
- Lutton Place
- Sch.
- ville Ter.
- PRESTON STREET
- Burial G?

BIOGRAPHIES

Team & Writers

Editor in Chief
MAGALI ROMÁN is an Argentinian novelist and editor based in Edinburgh. Born in Buenos Aires, she studied history and English literature in the United States before pursuing a master's degree in fiction at the University of Edinburgh. She writes fantastic fiction and is most inspired by writers like Silvina Ocampo, Haruki Murakami, Shirley Jackson, and Julio Cortázar.
Contact: www.magaliroman.com

Executive Editor
MEREL ELINE DE BEER (M.E. GERRETSEN) is a writer and historian from the Netherlands. She studied History at the University of Amsterdam and is currently doing her MSc in Creative Writing at the University of Edinburgh. She is interested in surrealism and magic realism, and through her writing likes to explore the bizarre and melancholy. She writes under the pen name M.E. Gerretsen.
Contact: merelelinedebeer@gmail.com

Art Director and Poetry Editor
ELSPETH REILLY holds a BA in Graphic Design from American University, and an MSc in Creative Writing with a focus in poetry from the University of Edinburgh. She was the art director for this publication, and hopes to continue to merge her two loves of creative writing and graphic design in the future.
Contact: elspethcreilly@gmail.com |
Instagram @drawspeth

Prose Editor
AMANDA-MARIE KALE is a California-based writer. Her writing has appeared in *The Collegian, Bits & Scraps, The Student Newspaper,* and *Cleaver Magazine.* She is actively

pursuing publication for her first novel.
Contact: amandamariekale7.wordpress.com |
Email amandamariekale@gmail.com

Prose Editor and Web Manager
NATASHA GRODZINSKI is a Canadian writer currently living and working in Edinburgh. Her writing is a result of too many summers spent in libraries, too many hours spent daydreaming, and the firm belief that the strangest stories are the best ones. Her work has appeared in *Three Drops From a Cauldron*.
Contact: natasha.grodzinski@gmail.com |
Twitter @TashGrodzinski

Prose Editor
MILAGROS LASARTE is Argentinian, though she has lived most of her life in France. In 2018 she graduated from the Sorbonne with a Bachelor in English (majoring in Literature). She is currently living in Edinburgh, completing a Master's Degree in Creative Writing, and is seeking agent representation for her first novel which is proudly finished and ready to find its readers. Her writing focuses on literary fiction and explores the complexity of the human psyche as well as the tension that arises from all that is left unsaid.
Contact: lasartemilagros@gmail.com

Prose Editor and Podcast Narrator
JOHN REID is a twenty-two-year-old Glaswegian writer. He was awarded the George Bruce Memorial Prize in 2018 from the University of Aberdeen and can also be found in the Electric Reads Young Writer's Anthology 2017.
Contact: johnareid1@virginmedia.com

Prose Editor
ELENA SIMS is a writer from Jacksonville Florida currently enrolled in the Creative Writing Masters program at the

University of Edinburgh. She has had work featured in online literary magazines such as *The Selkie* and *Pieces* and will be pursuing a PhD in English.
Contact: s1893013@ed.ac.uk

Prose Editor
KIRSTY SOUTER has a degree in English Literature and History from The University of Edinburgh, and has worked enough cleaning jobs that LinkedIn is convinced she has a bright future with Sodexo. She first rose to renown with celebrated poem 'Ten Purple Penguins' published in a Fife edition of *Playground Poets*. It's out of print, so you'll have to take her word for it that it was Burns calibre literature. Despite being editor of her school's diary in *The St Andrews Citizen* in 2013-2014, most believe 2005 was her peak.
Contact: *Instagram* @concerning_kj | *Twitter* @kirsty_souter

Prose Editor and Podcast Producer
WESTER WAGENAAR (1992) was born and raised in Groningen, the Netherlands, but lived abroad nearly half his adult life – he received a BA in Japan Studies and an MA in Euroculture studying at five universities in four countries. His creative writing focuses on the darker sides of the human condition, approached through diverse genres and from various angles. When Wester is not putting pen to paper, he spends his time playing games, fencing, and exploring cities in search of the cutest cats.
Contact: wester_w@hotmail.com | *Instagram* @qwesterw

Poetry Editor
ELLIE JACKSON. I am from Durham in the North East of England. I studied English at the University of Cambridge and studied Creative Writing (Msc) at The University of Edinburgh. I write poetry and create visual poetry, I am interested in the conversations between visual art and literary works.

I also write fiction.
Contact: ellie.jackson97@hotmail.co.uk

Poetry Editor and Proofreader
STEFANO PAPARO writes poetry.
Contact: sfpaparo@gmail.com

Poetry Editor
DEXTER YIM is an English teacher and editor in Hong Kong and graduated with a master's degree in Literary Studies from The Chinese University of Hong Kong. His poetry explores and zeros in on memory, nostalgia, alienation, loss and Hong Kong identities. His favourite writers are Haruki Murakami, George Orwell, Aldous Huxley and Kazuo Ishiguro. Hobby-wise, he is interested in photography, poetry, film studies and travelling.
Contact: dexterluckyim@gmail.com

Copy Editor
NICOLE CHRISTINE CARATAS is a Chicago-born fiction writer. She is currently based in Edinburgh.
Contact: nicole.caratas@gmail.com | *Twitter* @nicolecaratas

Proofreader
NICOLE HOOPER CAMPOS. As a result of dealing poorly with stress, Nicole has become a strong advocator of using bad experiences for fun story material. Now when things go bad, it's fine, because it might one day turn into that bestselling story. Originally from Florida, Nicole has spent much of her time moving from place to place trying to figure out life. She can often be found taking pictures of her adorable Jack Russell Terrier and posting them to their Instagram @pawingforadventures, in the hopes that one day he'll get a modeling contract and pay the bills so she can write full time.
Contact: nikkihoopercampos@yahoo.com

Proofreader

C. MARIS BOUNDS is an Arkansas-born, Indiana-raised writer. She currently lives in Edinburgh, Scotland (not Indiana, there is a difference).
Contact: marisbounds@aol.com|
Instagram @marisbounds | *Twitter* @ilike2gobymaris

Event Planner

ALYSSA OSIECKI is a writer, educator and all-around sassy lady with a very low tolerance for comfort zones. When she's not writing she's traveling, performing and consuming nearly inhuman quantities of pizza. Catch her blogging about expat life and other beautiful disasters at alyssaowrites.com or say hi at alyssaowrites@gmail.com.
Contact: alyssaowrites.com | alyssaowrites@gmail.com

Event Planner

JULIE GALANTE is a writer and visual artist. She was born in the US and called several European countries home before moving to Scotland in 2013. She is currently working on a short story collection about the uncanny, as well as a memoir about life as a young widow with immigration troubles. She holds an MBA in International Management, and loves to use her business skills to help creatives find their audiences and build sustainable practices. She lives in Edinburgh with her cat, Purrcules Mulligan.
Contact: juliegalante.com | *Instagram* @julie_galante | *Twitter* @julie_galante

Social Media Manager

SOPHIE LAY is a writer from Oxfordshire with a penchant for the queer and the beautiful. She has a first BA (Hons) in Creative Writing from the University of Gloucestershire. Her writing has previously been published in *Popshot Magazine,*

Bandit Fiction, and three of the University of Gloucestershire's *New Writing* Anthologies: *Reflections*, *Shadows*, and *Singularity*. She has also performed her flash fiction at both the Cheltenham Literature Festival and the Cheltenham Poetry Festival.
Contact: sophielay.wordpress.com | *Twitter* @Sophie_Lay

Writers

JAMES ALEX. Originally from the Scottish Borders, James Alex is a writer with interests in disability, technology, the social systems that surround us, and the way we interact with all of these things. All of his latest stories have involved the supernatural, something he is unsure of what to do about.
Contact: jamcpherson91@gmail.com | *Twitter* @xenorealisms

ALI MUSA AME. My nickname is 'King of Rhymes'. I am from Zanzibar. I write English and Swahili poems. I am studying MSc Creative writing at the University of Edinburgh. I am not published yet. I have been composing English and Swahili poems for 10 years in Zanzibar, mostly as a hobby and performance in ceremonies.
Contact: simba.asadu1@gmail.com | *Facebook* Ali Ame

MARC BERRY was born in Galashiels, Scotland and attended Hartwick College where he received his B.A in English Literature. Marc returned home to pursue a master's degree in Creative Writing at Edinburgh University.

NING CAI. Awarded the Singapore National Arts Council's Arts Scholarship to pursue her postgraduate studies at the University of Edinburgh, Ning Cai is a bestselling author and regular panelist at the annual Singapore Writers Festival. Her work has been nominated for prestigious Asian literary arts awards like the Singapore Literature Prize and the Epigram Books Fiction Prize. Her sixth book, *Manipulation*, the highly anticipated sequel to her popular YA crime novel, *Misdirection: The Savant Trilogy*, comes out this Autumn. Contact: NingCaiWrites@gmail.com | *Instagram*@Ning.Thing

ANGELO CASTIGLIONI. As it turned out, he is nothing like he imagined himself to be. A child of music, a student of psychology, and a sucker for absurdist fiction; Angelo seeks to untangle the cognitive dissonance of the post-internet generation through abstract storytelling. He writes to understand how best to live. He writes to understand how best to die. He writes because ambrosia tastes sweetest when sipped through a tiny reusable straw. On Tuesdays, Angelo can be found conversing with his cat about the nature of eternity or some other nonsense or perhaps not at all and he might be sleeping. Contact: angecastiglioni@gmail.com

ISSA DIOUME is a Franco-Senegalese writer born in Angers, France. From age five he was raised in India where he lived in a universal city dedicated to human unity, Auroville, for ten years. At fourteen he took his path and travelled to China and South Korea, where he played the game of Go competitively. His rich background, a deep love for languages, culture, and literature nourished his life until now. Therefore, he has many stories to tell and becoming a writer felt like the natural next step. Today he is completing an MSc in Creative Writing at the University of Edinburgh, in the hopes to hone his skills and give birth to many original tales and stories, and to be published and share with readers the benefits of his experiences. His current style is a spiced-up mélange of many, with

a penchant for magic-realism.
Contact: idioume@gmail.com |
Instagram @coffeewritingimproving

TINGYU LI is a Chinese comedian who tries to present China's funny face.
Contact: garfieldlty@hotmail.com | *Instagram* @garfieldlty

JOSH WAGNER is the author of five books, a few plays, and three graphic novels including the award-winning *Fiction Clemens* and *Pit Girl*. He likes to live as lightly and on-the-move as possible. Despite his growing obsession with the British Isles, Josh most often sets out from little ol' Missoula, Montana, which he is proud to call home.
Contact: www.joshwagner.xyz

IONA ZAWINSKI. I'm Iona Zawinski. I live in a caravan in East Lothian. I write stories, make music, and walk ma dog. I try tae make sense ay this thing – life – word by word. I like tae create a wee destination, tae carve oot a path tae it where before, there wasnae wan. It's too much tae contemplate – the vast cosmic tapestry – it's confusing, disheartening, kinday pointless and kinday necessary. I write fer the opportunity tae pick up wan thread, just the wan, and follow it aw the way tae the end. Gies me peace.
Contact: izawinski@gmail.com |
Facebook Iona Ismita Zawinski

A Note On The Design

The inspiration behind this cover design was vintage postcards— a memento, a snapshot in time. Despite us hailing from around the world, our pathways have intersected, and we all find ourselves studying at the same university, pursuing the same dream. When we look back at this book, a project we've all worked passionately and tirelessly on, we will be revisiting a year wherein we grew as writers, and as friends. The prose and poems within, having been written during our time together, will always transport us back to the moment of their creation (and their countless revisions). The book itself is a memento for our time spent together.

The colour palette is CMYK, a reference to the printing process: a medium that all those who are interested in writing and reading are keen to keep alive and thriving. These colors are eye-catching, and reminiscent of an Edinburgh sunset or sunrise.

Finally, the back cover was inspired by the flipside of a postcard. It is personalized with one of our incredible writers'— and our executive editor's—handwriting: Merel De Beer. Her handwriting adds a personal touch to an already very personal project. This a book signed from all of its contributors—we've all had our stamp on it.

Signed, sealed, delivered—it's now yours,

Elspeth Reilly, BA Graphic Design   *Elspeth Reilly*

From Arthur's Seat 4

First published in this edition by Egg Box Publishing in association with the University of Edinburgh as part of UEA Publishing Project.

International © 2019 retained by individual authors and artists. This book is sold subject to the condition that it shall not, by way of trade or otherwise, be lent, resold, hired out, stored in a retrieval system, or otherwise circulated without the publisher's prior consent in any form of binding or cover other than that in which it is published and without a similar condition including this condition being imposed on the subsequent purchaser.

Design and typesetting by Elspeth Reilly

Typeset in Times New Roman

www.fromarthursseat.com

Printed by Imprint Digital, UK.

Distributed by NBN International.

isbn 978-1-911343-95-0